Contents

A further worked example for Section 3 is available for download from the Heinemann website (see p. 186):

- Go to www.heinemann.co.uk/secondary
- Click on ICT
- Click on 16+ and select A level ICT (series), then Free Resources.

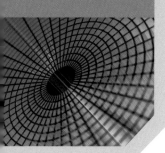

Introduction

This skills book has been devised to help you during the study of the AS module INFO1 in the GCE ICT level specification from AQA. It would also be useful to use during the study of any practical ICT skills course.

This book is a companion for the A level ICT for AQA text book, but can be used independently and for other ICT courses. It extends the suggestions for practical exercises in Unit 1 of that book, and looks at the process of successfully solving ICT problems.

The first section gives plenty of ideas for practical work, for using different input and storage devices appropriate to different situations, for using a myriad of different software packages to process the data captured and stored, and offers ideas for suitable presentation and dissemination methods.

By using show and tell methods, various software types are demonstrated, with advanced features of some of the familiar software packages and step-by-step demonstrations of some of the less mainstream options. These are bite-sized demonstrations, designed to offer a starting point for you to explore the facilities offered either by the package demonstrated or by a similar piece of software, enabling you to choose the most appropriate software for manipulating the type of data that you are working with.

The second section gives a wealth of ideas for practical exercises, always with appropriate use and the requirements of the examination module in mind. Contexts vary from small business problems to home and leisure problems, including some problems involving special requirements. We have given more than one option for each and a suggested best solution. These are meant to act as stimulus materials for you to follow, either as practice work or to be used as a basis for the problems that you will solve and take the evidence into the examination.

The third section has four worked example problems, each shown as a diary of events, followed by an example of the sample work required to be taken into the INFO1 exam. Not all solutions offer the best opportunities to show off the testing requirements of the unit, and so it might be advisable to prepare the Problem Definition material from one solution – perhaps a website or multimedia application – and the Test material from another – perhaps a spreadsheet or database solution.

At the end of this section there is also a selection of practice exam questions that might be asked about the work that you take in with you.

Jackie Rogers
Carl Lyon

Successful
Problem Solving
for AQA AS ICT Unit 1

Carl Lyon
Jackie Rogers

www.payne-gallway.co.uk

✓ Free online support
✓ Useful weblinks
✓ 24 hour online ordering

01865 888070

PAYNE-GALLWAY

Payne-Gallway is an imprint of Pearson Education Limited, a company incorporated in England and Wales, having its registered office at Edinburgh Gate, Harlow, Essex, CM20 2JE. Registered company number: 872828

www.payne-gallway.co.uk

Text © 2008 Jackie Rogers and Carl Lyon

First published 2008

12 11 10 09 08
10 9 8 7 6 5 4 3 2 1

British Library Cataloguing in Publication Data
A catalogue record for this book is available from the British Library

ISBN 978 1905 292 34 9

Typeset and illustrated by Sparks, Oxford
Produced by Sparks, Oxford
www.sparkspublishing.com

Cover design by Wooden Ark Studios
Cover photo © iStockPhotos

Printed in the UK by Scotprint

Websites
There are links to relevant websites in this book. In order to ensure that the links are up-to-date, that the links work, and that the sites are not inadvertently linked to sites that could be considered offensive, we have made the links available on the Heinemann website at www.heinemann.co.uk/hotlinks. When you access the site, the express code is 2394P.

Ordering Information
Payne-Gallway, FREEPOST (OF1771),
PO Box 381, Oxford OX2 8BR
Tel: 01865 888070
Fax: 01865 314029
Email: orders@payne-gallway.co.uk

Section 1
Skills

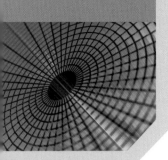

1.1 Capturing data and storing it

The first part of any successful ICT system is the input cycle. Getting data into the system is essential for the system to work. It is essential to enter data into the system in an accurate and timely manner to ensure that the system works correctly. To capture the data that is to be entered, and to make sure of its integrity, are the most important elements of a successful ICT system.

'Input' is any method of entering data into a system, using a variety of methods and a variety of mechanisms. Methods can be manual or automatic. Manual methods include the use of a keyboard, a scanning device, a mouse-click, a touch-screen or a microphone. Automatic methods include electronic file exchange and downloading from other sources, for instance a digital camera.

In the following diagram, the input peripheral is the device, such as the keyboard, the scanner or the mouse, used to input the data. The input sub-system is the method, or mechanism, which interprets the signal coming from the device and converts it into a form that the processor can understand, so that it can be stored appropriately.

Remote and intelligent data capture devices exist in all walks of life – digital cameras, PDAs, courier sign-for devices, meter reading devices, mobile phones and so on.

'Storage' is any method of holding data either temporarily or permanently, for instance Random Access Memory (RAM) is temporary storage, whereas a Hard Drive, a DVD-ROM, a Pen Drive or USB is permanent storage. Permanent storage holds the data when the computer is switched off.

Activity 1.1

- Make a list of all data capture devices that you have used in the past 7 days – include any at school, college, work, leisure (e.g. withdrawing cash, playing computer games and so on).

- Make a note of the type of data you captured and stored on each – text, numeric, audio, still image, video, etc.

1.1.1 Textual data

Text data is the simplest form of data for both capturing and storing. By text data, we normally mean any of the characters on the QWERTY keyboard, including letters, numbers and special characters such as ! ' £ $ % ^ & * () _ – + =.? < > { } [] @ #, and so on.

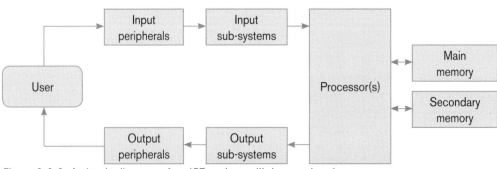

Figure 1.1.1 A simple diagram of an ICT system with human input

Each character is assigned a code for storage – most computers use either the ASCII or Unicode systems, where 7 or 8-bit patterns are used to signify the character, so storage space is relatively quite small. Most text-only files have sizes measured in kilobytes – even a 100-page document may be no more than a megabyte in size. Hence, storage of text files is simple – a floppy disk, at 1.44 megabytes capacity is usually big enough to take one or more text-only files.

The most common method of capturing text data is via typing the text into a keyboard, but there are other methods and variations.

A concept keyboard sends a signal to the computer to store a particular word or product code, where pictures or words are shown and the user presses them either using touch technology or a mouse. This saves the user typing time and the chance of making a typing error. A Braille keyboard has raised dots on the keys as an aid for the blind.

Likewise, clever design of input data capture forms will restrict user choice on some fields so a click of a mouse on the choice from the list or the radial or box next to the text required will also enable that text to be stored in the relevant field without having to type it in. Touch-screen technology can also be used to reduce typing text.

Voice input, using special software, such as Dragon Naturally Speaking, can also be used to capture text data for use, not only in word processing and other office-based applications, but also for writing emails, and for entering data into search engines. Latest versions claim up to 160 words per minute, approximately 3 times faster than the average computer user, and with 99% accuracy, it is a very viable option for anyone who hates typing, as well as those who may have developed RSI from too much keyboard or mouse use.

Optical character recognition allows freehand or hard-copy text to be converted into their electronic digital editable equivalent. Software, such as Textbridge, will take a printed page, scan it using a scanner and convert it into a document that can be edited in your favourite software.

One other storage issue to mention is to do with text objects, such as those created by Freehand or WordArt. While they can be edited, have size and fonts changed, etc., as normal text, they will be stored with a multitude of other data, indicating their shape and positioning, colour and size and so on, making the files much bigger.

1.1.2 Numeric data

Numeric data is treated in much the same way as text data when capturing and storing it in its simplest form. The characters 0–9 are merely characters on a keyboard or number pad.

Numeric keypads can be found on most PC keyboards, to the right of the main QWERTY keyboard, with alternatives on some laptops that do not have the space for a separate number pad. Calculators, combination door locks and telephones are other devices where you could expect to find a numeric keypad.

However, for numeric data to be processed as such, we have to look at the different ways that it can be stored – as binary numbers, as real numbers, as integers, as dates, as currency data, and so on.

Some software packages show numeric data only in its formatted display format. For instance, in Microsoft Access, a date is always shown in its DD/MM/YYYY format on input, query form and output. However, this is not how it is stored. It is stored as a single binary number taking up a single word of space instead of the 10 bytes of space if it were held as characters, indicating the number of days since a fixed date (on most PCs this is either 1st January 1900 or 1st January 1980, depending on the manufacturer).

Scanning methods are also used to capture numeric data. Magnetic ink recognition is used widely in banking situations to capture the numbers at the bottom of cheques. Optical mark recognition scans a document for marks which is converted into numeric equivalents for storage and processing.

Ultrasound scanners are used in medical and other areas and the results are held as numerical data which, when processed, can provide a visual representation of what has been scanned, and can also be electronically compared to previous data. Sonar scanners work in much the same way, converting the signals received into numerical data.

Sensory data capture, for example of temperature, speed or geologic movement, is captured as numeric data and used for many purposes, such as predicting weather change or imminent earthquakes.

1.1.3 Audio data

Sounds captured and stored on a computer system are referred to as audio data. This can be in the form of sound effects like screeching tyres, commentary (such as that provided by sports commentators) or music. Anything that can be heard and recorded is audio data.

The type of audio data required will dictate the type of data capture method chosen. For example a rock band will use a studio where they will plug their instruments into amplifiers and rely on sensitive microphones to detect the music being played or the lyrics being sung. The microphones are commonly linked to computer systems which sample the analogue sounds made and store the recording digitally as it is being played. Microphones detect sound waves and convert them into electronic signals that can be played back through appropriate equipment.

Alternatively, it is possible to produce tracks using just a computer system and music editing software. A popular option is to plug keyboards or drum machines, which transfer digital signals that are translated into musical sounds and notes, directly into the computer. Software can be purchased that can provide backing melodies or baselines which can be speeded up, slowed down or distorted. The musician can then add their own part of the track which is captured directly through the cables linking the instrument to the computer. If vocals are required, a microphone may still be used.

Activity 1.2

- Try to gain access to the software Audacity. It is a free to download audio editing file and instructions on how to use it follow in section 1.2.

- You will also need to download another piece of software called Lame MP3 Encoder V3.97; this is also free.

After the data is captured, it can be manipulated in a variety of ways to enhance the sound produced by the musicians. Each instrument may have been recorded individually. The sound artist will then take each recording and digitally stitch them together to create one track. The volume of each instrument can be adjusted so that one instrument does not drown out the others. Drum beats can be speeded up or slowed down and the lead singer's vocals can be distorted to create a different pitch or sound. The ultimate goal is to create a track that the intended audience will like.

The spoken voice is captured in a similar way. Audio books are achieved by asking someone to read a novel directly into a microphone. The microphone will be plugged into a computer system and sound recording software will be run which captures the spoken word in a digital format. This process can take several days and after the reading the publishers may wish to add sound effects at certain parts of the reading. A clap of thunder may follow the words 'and a wild storm suddenly struck the shore' or a short jingle may be played between each chapter. The extra sounds are captured in the same way as those mentioned above and are used to add atmosphere to the spoken word and the story being told.

The quality of the captured data will depend on the equipment and environment used to capture it. The evolution of audio capture means that microphones can now be plugged into computer systems and spoken into. Alternatively there are wireless options which do the same thing. The limitation of capturing quality audio is that microphones do not discriminate between what they record. A string of words spoken directly will be recorded, but so will the fire engine in the background rushing to an emergency or the sound of the cat knocking over a vase. To avoid noise pollution corrupting a recording, it is wise to make sure that it is done in a quiet place where no interruptions are likely to occur. This is why studio time is booked by musicians and audio books are read in special soundproof rooms.

Microphones come in a variety of shapes and sizes. Nowadays they are mostly wireless, removing the need to be physically attached to the computer. Headsets with microphones are used in call centres because they allow the user to hear and speak to the person at the other end of the call while they use a keyboard to make notes or search databases.

Activity 1.3

- Using the Internet, find 4 different examples of microphones.

- For each example state who the user might be and what they would use it for.

- Give details relating to cost, ease of use and any other special features included.

- Produce a poster to display your findings.

Activity 1.4

- The following are audio file extensions: .au, .mid, .ram, .wav and .mp3.

- Find out what software is required to process and play back the recording.

- Find 2 more audio file extensions and add them to your list.

1.1.4 Still image data

Still image data can come from many sources – original photographs and drawings, downloaded pictures and cartoons. How they are captured and how they are stored has repercussions on the quality of the image when it has been processed and when it is displayed.

Other methods for capturing audio data include using a dictaphone. This is a small, pocket-sized gadget which used to hold miniature cassette tapes and would be used to record interviews. Dictaphones now capture data digitally onto a small on-board storage device, which can then be easily transferred to a larger computer.

Similar technology is used in mobile phones which allow the user to make short videos with sound. Microphone technology is also used in hearing aids which capture and then amplify data so that the user can hear what is being said to them or what is going on around them. This is a very good example of input, processing and output working at a rapid beneficial rate.

All digital sound stored on a computer system is stored with a file extension, which gives a clue as to what software it can be played through and its quality.

Digital cameras are widely used to capture still images. They can be plugged directly into a system, or the flash card that stores the images can be plugged into a computer or Bluetooth® technology can be used to transfer the pictures from the camera to the computer. Each method will depend on the make and age of the camera. The newer models are more likely to utilise wireless technology and include advanced features to manipulate the data before it reaches the system. Most mobile phones now incorporate a camera and so images can be captured and stored, sent as MMS (Multimedia Messaging System) to other compatible phones, or sent as emails to anyone, anywhere in the world.

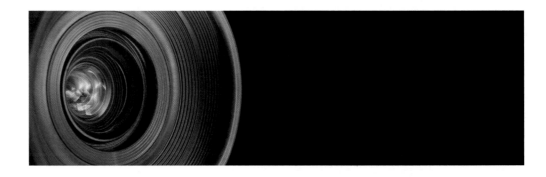

The amount of storage such an image requires depends on the digital camera used. The more pixels used to record the image, the more storage space is needed. The resolution of digital cameras and camera phones is often measured in megapixels. The term megapixel refers to the size and quality of an image. A megapixel refers to one million pixels. For example, a 2-megapixel camera can produce images with two million pixels. Since pixels are usually square and form a grid, a 1-megapixel camera will produce an image roughly 1200 pixels wide by 900 pixels high. By comparison, a VGA (Video Graphics Array) image (640 x 480 pixels) would be only 0.3 megapixels.

Megapixel images (1 megapixel or greater) are much larger than a phone display, so a megapixel camera will not make much difference compared to a sub-megapixel camera for phone-only applications such as MMS. Rather, megapixel cameras are useful for taking photos suitable for viewing on a PC and/or printing. Sub-megapixel cameras produce smaller images that only print well at very small sizes. Megapixel photos are larger in file size than sub-megapixel images, and so can take much longer, and consequentially cost more, to send wirelessly.

Most cameras and camera phones have an option to take photos at lower resolution (smaller size), if desired. This is useful for taking photos that will only be sent via MMS and not transferred to a PC or printed.

A photograph taken with a non-digital camera can be scanned in using a flatbed scanner, where the image is saved into a software application, from which it can be cropped, edited and enhanced. Many packages exist that perform image manipulation, some with rather more facilities than others. Look at Adobe Photoshop, Picasa, The GIMP, and also MS-Paint and the Windows Picture Editor.

Activity 1.5

- Scan in any photograph using one of the above image manipulation packages.

- Crop and enhance the image (eradicate red-eye, clean up any fuzziness, repair damaged areas, change the brightness etc.).

- Record the steps you took.

- Repeat with the same photograph and a second software package.

- Compare the two and decide which is easier to use.

Capturing non-photographic images can also be done using a scanner. An alternative is to use a drawing or graphic tablet and to save the original image for later use. Again, there are image manipulation packages that can be used to enhance or amend your drawing. The Macromedia suite of software has plenty of options for creating and manipulating both still and moving images.

Graphics tablets use a stylus instead of a pen on the flat surface with the resulting image appearing on a VDU (Visual Display Unit). A similar version of this technology is used on PDAs (Personal Digital Assistant), which translates the words and shapes, which are hand drawn on to the smaller screen, into actual text or sharper images.

Graphics tablets are most likely to be used for technical drawing and computer-aided design work. A still image of the design is created, with many layers, building up the whole picture. For instance, the design for a block of flats can be split into a drawing for each floor, with layers indicating the positioning of electrical and plumbing points, as well as internal features such as bathroom and kitchen designs. Each layer is an image in its own right and can be edited without touching or distorting the other layers.

Images can be stored for use on printed documents, such as photographs, combined with other data types (for instance, on a newsletter), or used on websites or on multimedia applications.

Activity 1.6

- Draw a coloured image of a house and garden on a piece of paper and scan it in. Note how much time this took.

- Use a drawing package to draw the same image, using the same colours. Note how long it took.

- Compare the two in terms of time taken and quality of image produced – which do you think is best?

Capturing moving data must not be confused with creating computer animations. Computer animations are built and manipulated within software and there is no specific data capture taking place. When the Shrek movies were being made, the film makers did not film a real ogre! However, prior to creating Shrek, the artist would have drawn him on paper before transferring the idea to a computer system. The fact remains that the drawing was not moving data until it was entered into software and manipulated.

For our purposes, moving images are those which are filmed and stored digitally. Images of reporters speaking live to camera from different parts of the world, recording the news as it happens, streamed into our homes and onto our computer screens is, nowadays, a normal occurrence.

Most moving image footage is captured for a desired purpose. That purpose tends to drive the capture device technology used. For example, speed cameras tracking the speed of approaching vehicles calculate the speed and take a picture if the car is going too fast. As they are targets of vandalism, the cameras have been designed to be relatively high up and robust to stop them being destroyed.

Mobile police units use portable speed cameras which compare readings from number plates with information in several national databases. The system is quickly able to inform the officers in the mobile unit if a car has been reported stolen, has no road tax or is uninsured, as well as working out if the driver is speeding or not.

CCTV (Closed Circuit Television) is another method of capturing moving images. The purpose in this case depends on the positioning of the camera. Shopping centres use them to monitor customers while they shop and track suspicious looking shoppers up to the point where they leave the store. Much of what is filmed is stored digitally. This means sections can be recalled by running search criteria relating to times and dates when a crime or other activity took place.

Activity 1.7

- Using the Internet, find 2 case studies of where moving image data capture took place.

- For each example state what the purpose of the data capture was and what technology was used.

- What, if any, were the resulting outcomes from capturing the data?

Domestic users use digital video cameras to record the birth of their children, parties, weddings, and other family occasions. Teachers could produce videos of pupils displaying the results of research which could be used as revision material, rather than a book, prior to exams. Doctors could film a complex operation and provide a commentary afterwards to act as training material for aspiring surgeons.

The media for data capture has evolved beyond the need to use standard video tape and fits into quite tiny hand-held video camera units.

Moving image data capture technology has been developed to recognise human beings too. Key measurements are taken around a person's face and stored in a database. Using similar technology to the number plate recognition system mentioned earlier, police are able to point the camera at individuals and get the computer system to work out who they are. Of course, this will only work if their details are already known and in the database. In the UK, many people already have their images digitally stored on either the UK passport authority database or the Driving and Vehicle Licence Authority database.

Activity 1.8

- Carry out research to find a popular brand of home video camera currently available on the market.

- Produce details of any features it includes and how it is different from previous versions of home video cameras.

All moving filmed digital data is stored with a file extension which dictates its quality and what software it can be edited on or played through.

Activity 1.9

- The following are motion picture file extensions: .avi, .mov and .mpg.

- Write a brief description for each including details of any related software.

- Find 2 more motion picture file extensions and provide brief details.

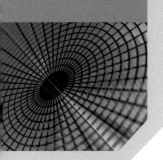

1.2 Manipulating data and transferring it

1.2.1 Introduction to types of data and possible tools

There are several different types of data which can all be manipulated and transformed into meaningful information.

Text and numbers

Text and number data is that which is read and appears in many sizes, styles and colours. Books, newspapers, information leaflets and instruction manuals are all a result of combining different letters into words to form sentences that make sense and are useful to the reader. Text is used to help describe a situation and to provide advice, news and directions.

Being able to order text and numbers to create a meaningful output is common practice for most people who own a personal computer system. After the machine is switched on text is often required to allow a user to log on, open an email account, respond to emails, use a search engine and to access other online facilities. Word processors, desktop publishing packages, presentation packages, spreadsheets and database packages all make use of text and numeric data as a prime form of data held and manipulated.

Still images

Still images represent a picture that displays a certain product, person or scene. Images are often used with text in order to reduce the number of words required to describe something. Often an image on its own can be inspiring, while others need a caption to help explain what it means. An image could be a simple shot of a doorway. Like this it is fairly meaningless. A caption of only a few words, such as 'the entrance to the Prime Minister's house' gives the image more meaning.

Images can also be used to keep a record of how someone or something changes over time. Each image is merely a split second of an occasion at a specific moment. Many families can produce a string of photographs that show how they and their children have grown up and changed. Images can help to clarify situations too. For example, the police will use images to help try to identify suspects. An accurate representation of a suspect may be difficult to obtain from a victim's description, but by showing the victim an image, the chances of obtaining a clear description are increased. In some cases this leads to an arrest.

Drawing packages range from those simple enough to be used by primary age children to complex computer-aided design packages used by architects and engineers. They all produce a still image. Web designers and advertising technicians use advanced drawing packages to produce images for use in adverts, on posters or on websites.

Photographic images can be captured, then manipulated using specialist software packages, so that the published photograph looks quite different from the original.

Moving images and animation

This type of data is a step up from still images which only capture a fraction of any given time. Moving images capture a period of time. The movement may last for one second or several hours. The capturing equipment will dictate how long the moving image process will last. Captured live movement can then be manipulated with any number of movie editing packages.

Animation is created on a computer system and is not captured in the same way as filming real life. Animated data can be used to represent characters and carry out tasks that humans cannot perform for physical or safety reasons.

There are a range of options that can use or create animation, ranging from simple basic animation packages (which some schools already have) to the more expensive options similar to those used by Disney and other Hollywood animators.

Sound

Data in the form of sound means that those who cannot see text or still or moving images can still hear a description of a scene or situation. Sound is also meaningless until it has been processed, edited, reduced or increased, turned up or down, and cropped.

Audio data is captured in sound files and often mixed with other types of data to help crystallise the message to be broadcast. Images can be given captions which are read out loud, moving images often have a commentary placed over scenes of natural wonder, and animated characters are given voices laced over their screen images.

Processing tools

With so much data available it is necessary to have devices on which to store, process and view it. Home computers, super computers, mainframes and servers all provide access to reams of data. There are a myriad of software packages available on these machines that allow data manipulation and presentation.

PDAs, mobile phones and MP3 players are other devices used to access and view processed data. Most hold chips and processors, and have some limited software which enables the user to process and convert the original data into something completely different.

Keyboards, spinning dials, touch-screens, buttons and voice activation provide the gateway from which data can be viewed, saved and converted to suit the need of the individual. Data is perceived as such a valuable commodity that it is accessible on demand from trains, boats, roads and planes via satellite links.

Computer technology means that where there is a connection to the Internet, there is also the possibility to access data from around the world and thus to cut, combine and transform files, containing tracks and motion, to create something completely different, with an alternative message. The Internet allows published data to travel around a Wide Area Network and means it can be made available to an audience of millions.

Satellite navigation systems, printers of all shapes and sizes, multimedia home centres, robots and industrial machinery all allow data to appear to seamlessly flow throughout their circuitry and give outputs according to the needs of the operator.

The power to process raw data into meaningful information by smart technological minds and sophisticated machines is set to become more widespread. Home refrigerators can now announce that they are low on milk and washing machines can set the most economical and appropriate wash based on the fabric placed within the drum. Domestic machines can already be networked so that the refrigerator can automatically link to a supermarket system and place the next order and arrange a delivery time. The next level might be a series of data travelling through the same network which allows all intelligent machines to communicate with one another.

1.2.2 Word-processing software

The instructions and examples given use Microsoft Word 2007. Older versions of MS Word have the same functions available, as will OpenOffice Writer, as well as many other word-processing packages.

It is assumed that AS-level students can use a word-processing package to a fairly high level by this time, so the emphasis of this section is to show some of the more advanced features that will help you to create a professional looking document for your client, your teacher or yourself.

Using Table of Contents (TOC)

Start with a document that has different levels of headings in it. You can go back through a document and add heading styles at appropriate places if you haven't got an appropriate document to use. Here is an example from the A level ICT for AQA book. Note how the different headings have been used throughout the sample section – three heading levels in total, Heading styles 1, 2, and 3.

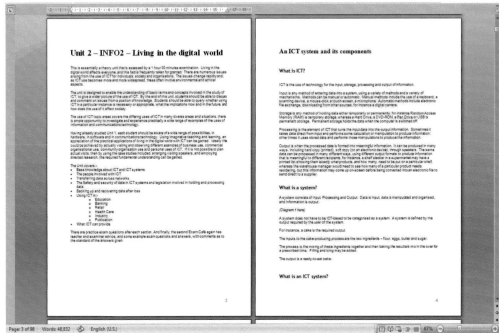

Figure 1.2.1 Formatted text

Figure 1.2.2 References tab showing Table of Contents group

Under the **References** tab, there is a **Table of Contents** (TOC) group that includes a TOC icon. Make sure the cursor is positioned where you want the TOC to be inserted (generally at the beginning of the document), choose a style from the options given (these can be modified) and press **OK**. The first attempt shows that there are some formatting problems within the text as the TOC function has picked up some narrative lines that should not be headings.

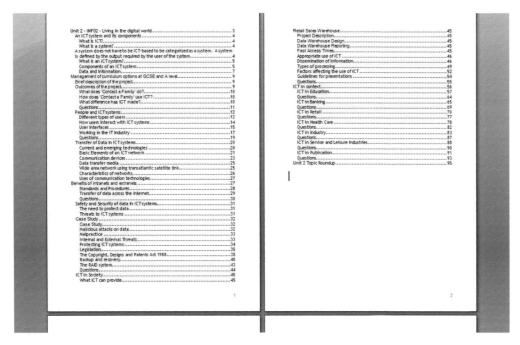

Figure 1.2.3 First draft Table of Contents

Figure 1.2.4 Update TOC dialog box

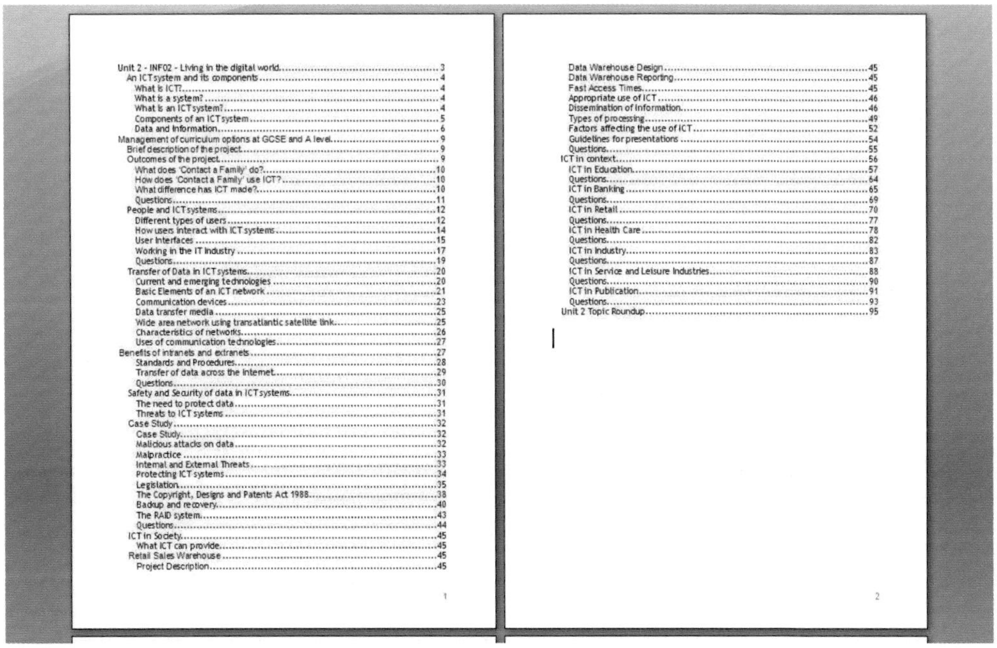

Corrections are made within the body and the TOC can be updated by right-clicking within the table, choosing the **Update** field and then following the instructions in the dialog box that appears (Figure 1.2.4).

Choose **Update entire table** to tidy up the unwanted entries and all page numbers will adjust to their correct places as shown in Figure 1.2.5.

Figure 1.2.5 Final Table of Contents

Using Indexes

Figure 1.2.6 Reference tab showing Index group

In the **Index** group there is an **Insert Index** icon that can be selected to create an index. However, to enable this function to be carried out you first have to work through your document marking up entries to be included in the index.

To do this, highlight a word, or phrase that you want to go into the index, then press **Alt**, **Shift** and **X** to view the following dialog box.

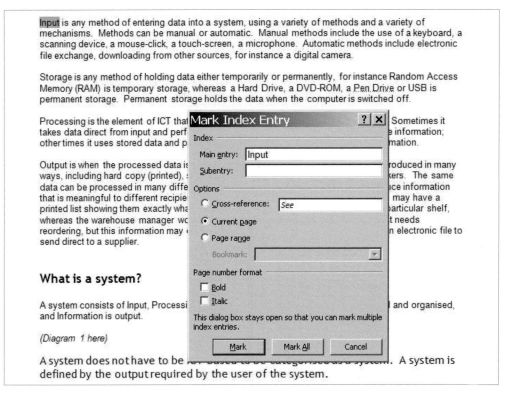

Figure 1.2.7 Mark Index Entry

You can see that the highlighted word has appeared in the **Main entry** field. Choose **Mark All** if you wish every occurrence of the word or phrase to appear in the Index. Beware that the index will use the formatting associated with the first instance of the word i.e. the one you highlighted, although that can be adjusted once the index is created.

The marked up text looks like Figure 1.2.8 – note that all formatting is shown while this process is underway – you can remove it when you are finished.

What·is·a·system⟦·XE·"system"·⟧·?·¶

A·system⟦·XE·"system"·⟧·consists·of·Input⟦·XE·"Input"·⟧,·Processing⟦·XE·"Processing"·⟧·and·Output·
XE·"Output"·⟧··Data⟦·XE·"Data"·⟧·is·input,·data·is·manipulated·and·organised,·and·Information⟦·XE·
"Information"·⟧·is·output.¶
¶

Figure 1.2.8 Marked up text

Once you are happy that you have included all of the words or phrases that should be in the index, position the cursor where you want the index to be inserted (normally at the end of the document) and then choose **Insert Index** from the **Index** group and you will get a dialog box like the one shown in Figure 1.2.9.

Various options are available – one or more columns, page number positioning and so on. Choosing a single column and **Indented** results in an index that looks like Figure 1.2.10.

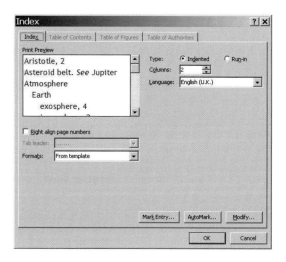

Figure 1.2.9 Index dialog box

```
INDEX¶
¶
¶
communication·links,·5,·88¶
Data,·1,·2,·4,·5,·7,·9,·17,·22,·25,·27,·31,·33,·36,·37,·38,·43,·48,·49,·54,·64,·90,·91,·
    97,·100,·101¶
hardware,·3,·5,·6,·7,·13,·14,·15,·27,·35,·36,·37,·39,·54,·55,·56,·74,·100,·101¶
Information,·1,·2,·3,·4,·7,·8,·9,·47,·50,·55,·84,·86,·100¶
Input,·4,·7,·100¶
Output,·4,·7,·100¶
people,·3,·5,·6,·8,·9,·10,·14,·15,·16,·18,·19,·20,·21,·22,·26,·29,·30,·33,·34,·35,·36,·
    37,·40,·41,·43,·46,·49,·50,·52,·57,·69,·70,·71,·72,·75,·76,·78,·80,·81,·82,·83,·86,·
    89,·92,·93,·97,·98,·100¶
peripherals,·5,·6,·25¶
power·supplies,·5¶
procedures,·5,·25,·27,·35,·36,·39,·43,·45,·47,·54,·82,·83,·85,·100,·101¶
Processing,·4,·6,·53,·54,·55,·100¶
software,·3,·5,·6,·10,·13,·14,·15,·17,·18,·19,·20,·25,·26,·27,·28,·29,·35,·36,·37,·40,·
    41,·49,·55,·56,·57,·58,·60,·61,·62,·70,·75,·76,·77,·78,·82,·86,·88,·90,·91,·92,·93,·
    96,·97,·98,·99,·100,·101¶
Storage,·4,·6,·100¶
system,·1,·4,·5,·6,·7,·8,·9,·10,·11,·13,·14,·15,·16,·17,·18,·19,·23,·24,·25,·30,·33,·34,·
    35,·36,·37,·39,·40,·41,·43,·44,·45,·46,·47,·48,·49,·52,·53,·54,·55,·58,·60,·63,·65,·
    70,·71,·73,·75,·76,·77,·80,·82,·83,·84,·85,·86,·88,·89,·92,·93,·98,·100¶
¶
```

Figure 1.2.10 Final index

Using Tables

A table is a useful way to show many items in a word-processed document and most students will have used them previously. There are just one or two functions within the Table feature that are worth learning to ensure your document looks professional.

In Word 2007, choose **Table** from the **Insert** tab and insert a table that resembles that in Figure 1.2.11. Once the table is inserted the **Design** ribbon will be shown which offers options for the table design.

However the **Layout** tab is where you will find the advanced options.

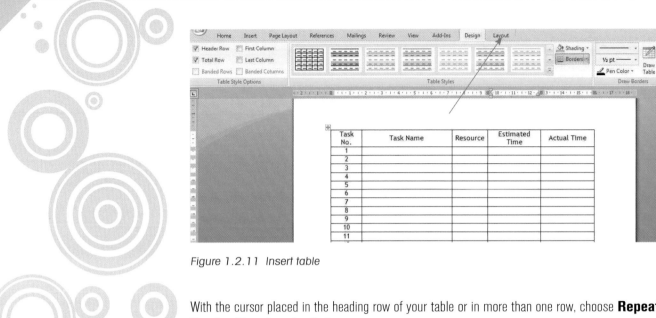

Figure 1.2.11 Insert table

With the cursor placed in the heading row of your table or in more than one row, choose **Repeat Header Row** from the **Data** group.

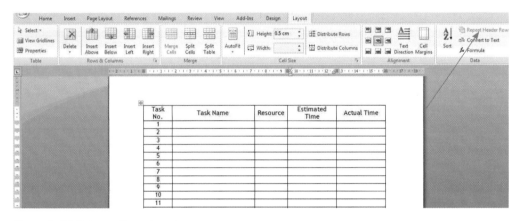

Figure 1.2.12 Repeating a header row

This automatically repeats the heading row when the table goes over to another page.

44				
45				
46				

1

Task No.	Task Name	Resource	Estimated Time	Actual Time
47				
48				
49				

Figure 1.2.13 Heading row repeated

The other useful function is the ability to add formulas to the table, for instance to allow it to add up a column of figures. Again, make sure that the cursor is on the box where you need the formula to be inserted and choose **Table** > **Layout** > **Formula**.

In the dialog box that appears, type in a formula (you can use any mathematical formula that you would use in a spreadsheet package, such as Sum, Average, etc.) or use the drop-down menu under the **Paste function** field (Word automatically inserts the command (ABOVE)), choose the format that the number should take and click **OK**.

This is not as sophisticated as a similar spreadsheet function, but can be useful for simple tabulations where it is not required to set up a new spreadsheet.

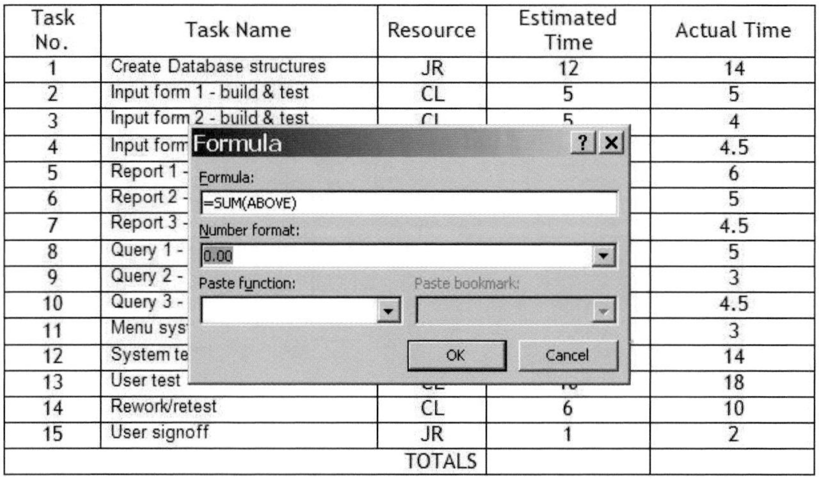

Figure 1.2.14 Insert formula

Once the formulas have been inserted, they will not automatically update if you change any of the rows in the table. If rows are changed, you need to right-click in the cell with the formula and press the **Update** field to adjust the total.

Task No.	Task Name	Resource	Estimated Time	Actual Time
1	Create Database structures	JR	12	14
2	Input form 1 - build & test	CL	5	5
3	Input form 2 - build & test	CL	5	4
4	Input form 3 - build & test	CL	5	4.5
5	Report 1 - Build & test	CL	5	6
6	Report 2 - Build & test	CL	5	5
7	Report 3 - Build & test	CL	5	4.5
8	Query 1 - build & test	JR	5	5
9	Query 2 - build & test	JR	4	3
10	Query 3 - build & test	JR	4	4.5
11	Menu system	CL	5	3
12	System test	JR	10	14
13	User test	CL	10	18
14	Rework/retest	CL	6	10
15	User signoff	JR	1	2
	TOTALS		87.00	102.50

Figure 1.2.15 Completed table

A further feature is the ability to make a chart from the table data. Choose **Chart** on the **Insert** ribbon and choose your preferred style of chart or graph and click **OK**. A new window will appear where you can cut and paste data from your table into the chart area.

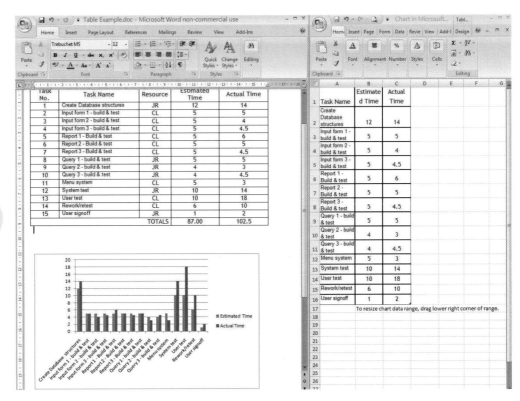

Figure 1.2.16 Constructing the chart

The resulting chart from our table of data looks like this:

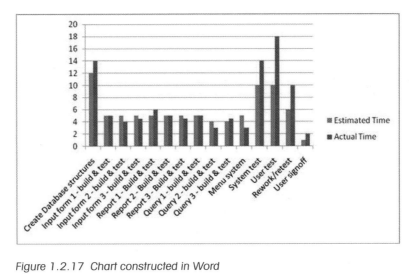

Figure 1.2.17 Chart constructed in Word

Creating templates

There are many elements to creating a template – headers, footers, a watermark, a style and perhaps some standard text. Having these already predefined in a document will save time when creating similar documents over and over again.

Inserting a watermark (faint text or an image that lies on every page) can be a useful way to protect your documents. Companies often use this to stamp 'Draft' or 'Specimen' on pages that they expect to change in later versions to avoid the wrong information being used.

From the **Page Layout** ribbon, choose **Watermark** from the **Page Background** group. There are some standard choices that you could insert, or you can choose to create a custom watermark. This brings up the following dialog box. Complete the required fields and click **OK**.

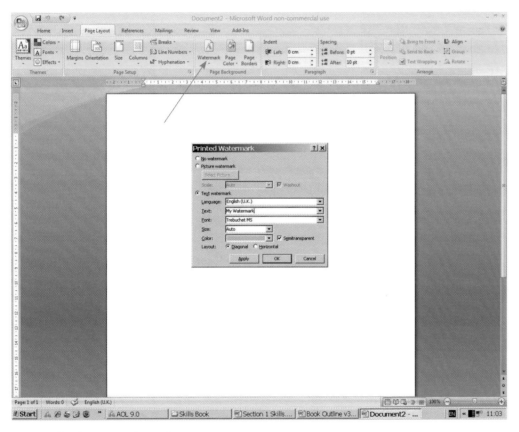

Figure 1.2.18 Insert watermark

You cannot see the watermark in **Edit** mode, but it will show in **Print Preview**.

Figure 1.2.19 Displayed watermark

Headers, footers and page numbers are added through the **Header & Footer** group on the **Insert** ribbon. Once you have chosen a style, there are then various options for formatting each on the **Design** ribbon.

Figure 1.2.20 Header and Footer options

Page formatting options can be found on the **Page Layout** ribbon.

Figure 1.2.21 Page Layout ribbon

Inserting static fields *in situ* – both automatically updated fields, such as dates, and fields that need to be manually updated when using the template – can save time. Once your template has all of these features included as required, use **Save As** to save the template for future use by saving as a Word Template in the **Save as type** field.

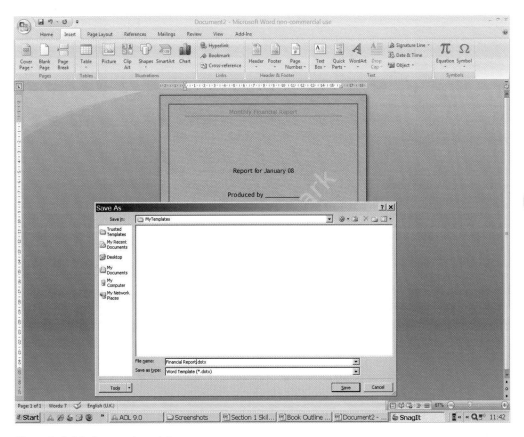

Figure 1.2.22 Save as template

Mail Merge

Using the **Mailings** menu it is easy to create a mail merged letter or set in motion an envelope or label printing run, all using an existing or new data source.

For a letter:

Set up the main document and save it.

Choose **Select Recipients** from the **Start Mail Merge** group and choose **Use Existing List** which will require you to locate a data source, generally a spreadsheet or database of details.

Once your data source is chosen and edited if necessary, add merge fields using the **Insert Merge Field** option from the **Write and Insert Fields** group. Remember to put a space between fields on the same line, for instance between title and surname.

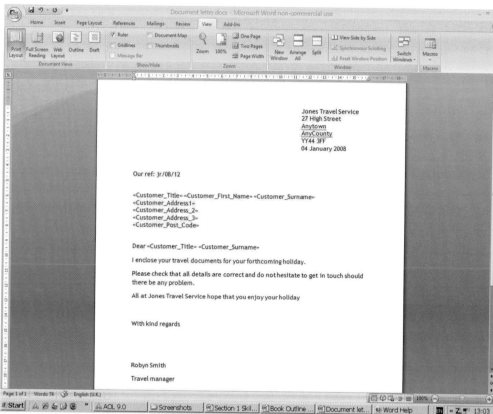

Figure 1.2.23 Merge document

Choose **Edit Recipients** to choose exactly which records from the data source are required for the merge. Choosing **Finish and Merge** from the **Finish** group gives you options to print everything that has been merged, to send email messages or to edit the individual merged documents. This last option then gives further possibilities on what to merge – all records, just one record or a range.

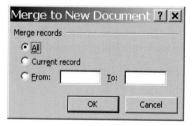

Figure 1.2.24 Merge options

The final merged document will have as many pages as there are records on the data source. It can be amended, saved and printed as required.

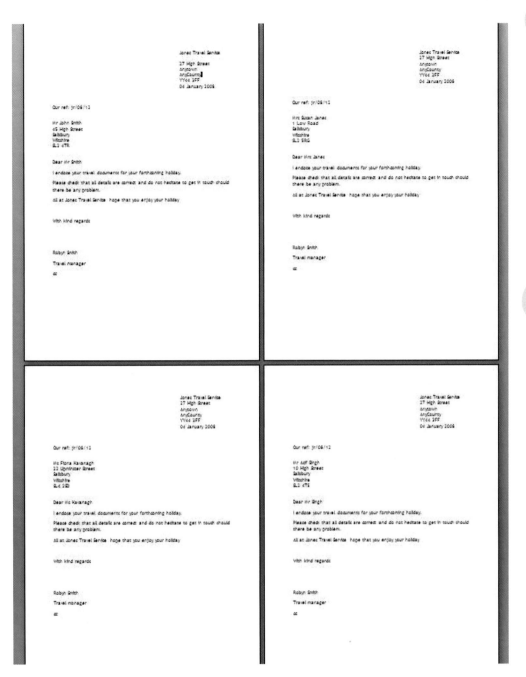

Figure 1.2.25 Merge results

1.2.3 Spreadsheet software

Instructions and examples are using Microsoft Excel 2007. Older versions of MS Excel should have the same functions available, as will many other spreadsheet packages.

It is assumed that AS-level students can use a spreadsheet package to a fairly high level by this time, so the emphasis of this section is to show some of the more advanced features and functions that will help you to produce a client-usable spreadsheet. Here is a collection of useful tips for using Excel 2007.

Macros

It is easier to create, record and work with macros when the **Developer** ribbon is available. From the **Microsoft Office** button, choose **Excel Options** at the bottom of the panel and click the third option – **Show Developer tab in the Ribbon** – and then click **OK**.

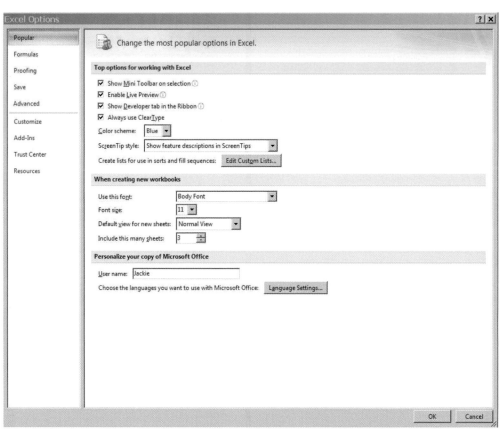

Figure 1.2.26 Excel Options

The **Developer** ribbon is then added. From here, all actions are easily accessible for controlling macro and VBA editing.

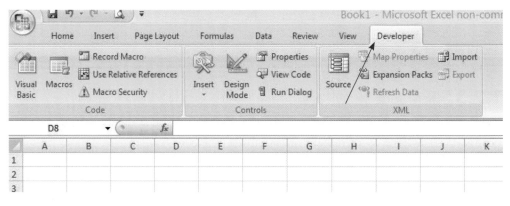

Figure 1.2.27 Developer menu

Whilst developing your macro and VBA work, it is advisable to enable all macros. This can be done by clicking on **Macro Security** in the **Code** group and choosing the options to allow all macros.

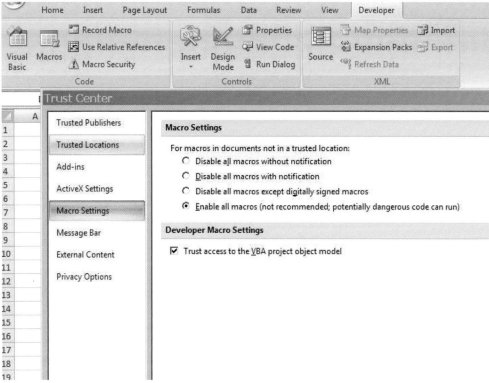

Figure 1.2.28 Trust Center

Please remember to reset these options, especially if you are on a shared machine or network, when you are finished.

Protecting worksheets

Having been briefed to produce a spreadsheet application for a client, before it's put into operation by them you must be careful to protect any static data from accidental overwrite by users. To do this you can simply hide an area of the worksheet, or even a whole sheet in a workbook.

The **Format** menu, found in the **Cells** group on the **Home** tab, gives options to hide and unhide rows, columns and sheets, an opportunity to lock cells so that their contents can't be changed, and an opportunity to protect the whole sheet or workbook, with or without a password. These are sensible actions to take to prevent an inexperienced user from accidentally changing important data or overwriting formulas you have entered into cells.

In fact, hiding worksheets is a professional action – there is no need for a user to see data that is not relevant to their use of the application. Clever final construction of a spreadsheet application can allow it to be used for more than one purpose.

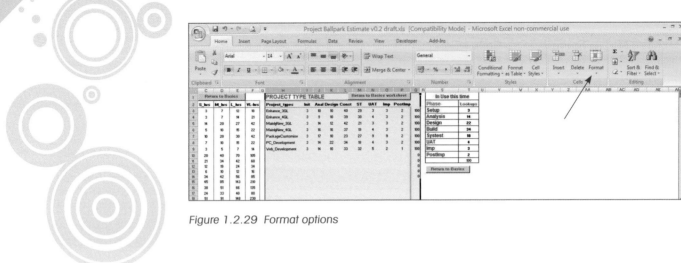

Figure 1.2.29 Format options

Using named areas

Using names can make it easier to understand the purpose of a cell reference (a cell reference is the set of coordinates that a cell occupies on a worksheet. For example, the reference of the cell that appears at the intersection of column B and row 3 is B3), constant (this is a value that is not calculated. For example, the number '210' and the text 'Quarterly Earnings' are constants. An expression, or a value resulting from an expression, is not a constant), formula (this is a sequence of values, cell references, names, functions, or operators in a cell that, together, produce a new value. A formula always begins with an equal sign, '='), or table (a table is a collection of data about a particular subject that is stored in records (rows) and fields (columns)), each of which may be difficult to understand at first glance. Using names also makes referencing from other places in the workbook easier as there is no need to remember cell ranges, or to add the sheet name. The named range could also be moved, by the insertion or deletion of rows or columns around the area, but there would be no need to manually change any reference.

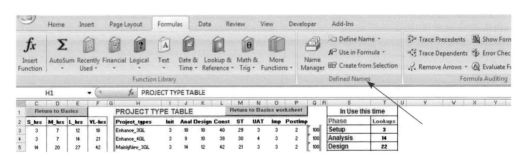

Figure 1.2.30 Defined Names

Access to the naming tools is from the **Defined Names** group on the **Formulas** ribbon. Names can be defined as having scope in just one worksheet (sheet1, sheet2, etc.) or in the whole workbook. Using the latter also makes it easier to navigate around the workbook – by simply choosing the named range to jump to, Excel positions itself straight there.

Here is an example. In the following workbook the **Defined Name** 'Analysis?' was chosen from a drop-down list on the **Formulas** bar with the Models worksheet active, and the workbook immediately jumped to cell B32 on the Basics worksheet.

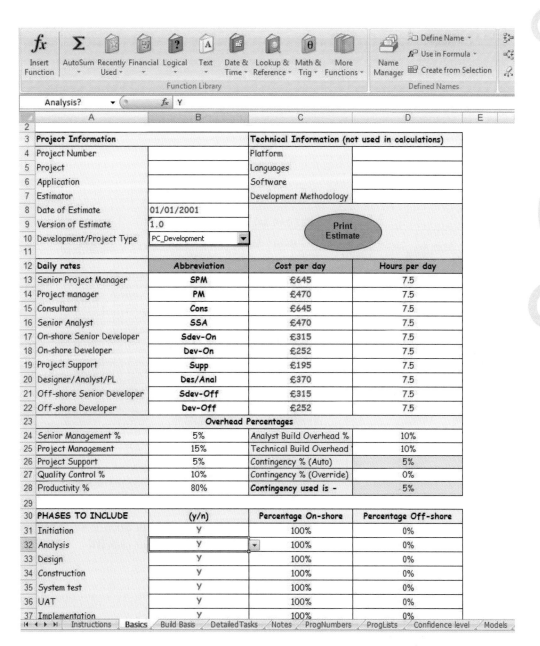

Figure 1.2.31 Named cell B32

As well as being useful for clarity and understanding of data, names are useful for future spreadsheet development as they can be assigned to cells containing all sorts of data – references, constants, formulae or even a complete table of data – which would be difficult to remember without a name.

Example type	Example with no name	Example with a name
Reference	=SUM(D20:D30)	=SUM(ThirdQuarterSales)
Constant	=PRODUCT(A3,17.5)	=PRODUCT(Price, VAT)
Formula	=SUM(VLOOKUP(A1,B1:F20,5,FALSE), – G5)	=SUM(Stock_Level, – Order_Amount)
Table	H4:H36	=TopSales08

Pivot tables

Pivot tables (or pivot table reports) and pivot charts are used to make sense of tabular data in a spreadsheet.

Use a pivot table report to summarise, analyse, explore, and present summary data. Use a pivot chart report to visualise this summary data in a pivot table report, and to easily see comparisons, patterns, and trends.

Starting with some tabular data, such as that shown below . . .

	A	B	C	D	E	F	G	H	I	J
1					**FLEET CAR SALES**					
2	Date	Order No	Customer	Car Make	Car Model	Quantity	Retail Price - Per Car	Sales Price - Per Car	Total Sales Price	
3	01/09/2008	1007	BT	BMW	316i	10	£15,000.00	£10,000.00	£100,000.00	
4	02/09/2008	2569	ELS	Vauxhall	Vectra	5	£13,000.00	£8,500.00	£42,500.00	
5	02/09/2008	4590	British Gas	Ford	Fiesta Van	10	£10,000.00	£6,500.00	£65,000.00	
6	03/09/2008	1239	Selfridges	Audi	A3	5	£17,000.00	£11,500.00	£92,000.00	
7	03/09/2008	2350	CIS	BMW	316i	30	£15,000.00	£10,000.00	£300,000.00	
8	04/09/2008	4520	ICL	BMW	316i	20	£18,000.00	£12,000.00	£240,000.00	
9	01/09/2008	3421	ICL	Ford	Fiesta Van	20	£10,000.00	£6,500.00	£130,000.00	
10	02/09/2008	4778	TES	Vauxhall	Corsa	25	£8,000.00	£5,500.00	£137,500.00	
11	02/09/2008	4929	Dillons	Audi	A3	25	£17,000.00	£11,500.00	£287,500.00	
12	06/09/2008	1769	Parcel Force	Ford	Fiesta Van	40	£10,000.00	£6,500.00	£260,000.00	
13	03/09/2008	3789	Parcl Force	Peugeot	306	40	£12,000.00	£7,000.00	£280,000.00	
14	04/09/2008	2765	CIS	Peugeot	306	50	£12,000.00	£7,000.00	£350,000.00	
15	11/09/2008	4436	Whitbread	Audi	A3	60	£17,000.00	£11,500.00	£690,000.00	
16	12/09/2008	2891	G&M Leisure	Citroen	Asara	15	£16,000.00	£11,000.00	£165,000.00	
17	07/09/2008	4567	G&M Leisure	Audi	A3	15	£17,000.00	£11,500.00	£172,500.00	
18	09/09/2008	2401	Dillons	Peugeot	306	30	£12,000.00	£7,000.00	£210,000.00	
19	21/09/2008	4326	ICL	Ford	Fiesta Van	10	£10,000.00	£6,500.00	£65,000.00	
20										
21										
22										
23										

Figure 1.2.32 'Fleet Car Sales' data

. . . highlight the full data table, and then select **PivotTable** from the **Tables** group on the **Insert** ribbon. Choose to either position the pivot table on this sheet or a new one, and click **OK**.

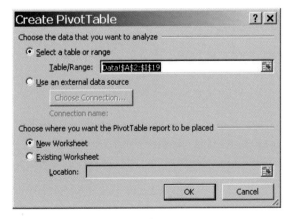

Figure 1.2.33 Create PivotTable options

An empty design sheet appears with a design panel on the right hand side of the screen to make choosing the fields required easier. Changing fields will change the pivot table report as seen here.

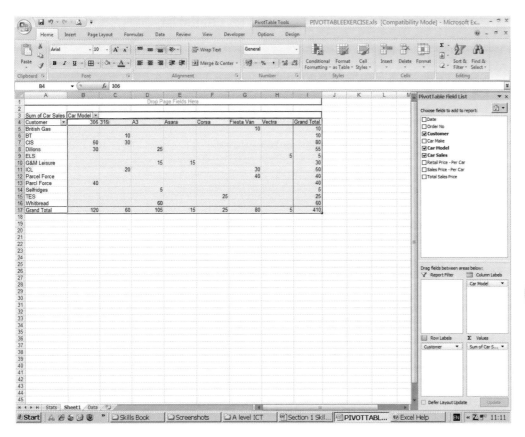

Figure 1.2.34 Pivot table report

To create a pivot table chart at the same time as the pivot table report, select **PivotChart** from the **PivotTable** menu and follow the steps for putting the data into the table as above. Once created, both report and chart can be edited in the normal way.

1.2.4 Database software

Again, it is assumed that AS students have used database software previously, so know the basics and beyond of creating tables, forms, queries and reports.

Open source database software such as MySQL is available free of charge, though these programs tend to be used by quite technically-minded students, as the user-interface is not set out to be as user-friendly as the more commercial packages. The examples used here can be used with Microsoft Access 2000, 2003, XP, 2007 and Access 2007 Runtime. The Runtime version allows users of a database management solution built in Access to run the application without having the full version of Access installed on their systems. The Runtime version is available free of charge.

Using the 'Not In List' function

If using a runtime version of a database management solution, the end-user is not usually able to customise it. However by using the 'not in list' function, users are able to make additions to a value list in a combo box. There may have been a finite set of values when the list was first set up, but as more, equally valid, options appear over time, you may wish to allow the user to add the new values to the underlying table.

This case would call for you to make use of the combo box's **NotInList** event.

Firstly, there are certain properties that need to be pre-set:

■ The combo box must have its **RowSource** set to either a table or a query (not a value list or a field list).

■ The combo box must have the **RowSourceType** set to **Table/Query**.

■ You must set the **LimitToList** property to **Yes**. (The event will only be triggered if this property is set.)

The following input form has all of the properties set as defined above.

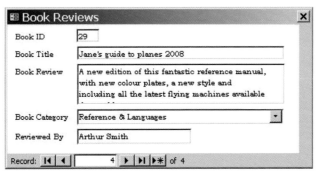

Figure 1.2.35 Input form

The **Book Category** field is based on a table containing a range of values for category, but the one value required by the user is not among them. By typing the new value into the combo box, the following message is seen.

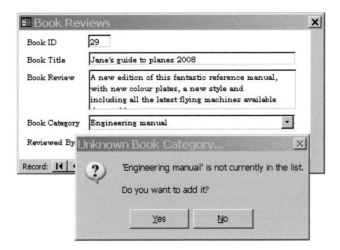

Figure 1.2.36 NotInList dialog box

This dialog box is triggered by the following code (cboBookCategory), added to the combo box **NotInList** event using code builder:

```
Private Sub cboBookCategory_NotInList(NewData As String, Response As Integer)
  Dim strSQL As String
  Dim i As Integer
  Dim Msg As String

  ' Exit this sub if the combo box is cleared
  If NewData = "" Then Exit Sub

  Msg = "" & NewData & "'  is not currently in the list. " & vbCr & vbCr
  Msg = Msg & "Do you want to add it?"

  i = MsgBox(Msg, vbQuestion + vbYesNo, "Unknown Book Category …")
  If i = vbYes Then
    strSQL = "Insert Into tblBookCategories ([strBookCategory]) " & _
      "values ('" & NewData & "'); "
    CurrentDb.Execute strSQL, dbFailOnError
    Response = acDataErrAdded
  Else
    Response = acDataErrContinue
  End If
End Sub
```

This will add the new value to the combo box and allow it to be assigned to the record.

Once 'Yes' is chosen, the new value will be allowed and added to the table for book categories. It will therefore be in the list presented for any further data entry.

Combining combo boxes

It is often the case that you want to restrict the options in one combo box depending on what has been selected in another.

For instance, an application has the following two Microsoft Access tables:

tblStore
StoreID (Primary Key)
StoreName

tblStore

StoreID	StoreName
1	M&S
2	Tesco
3	Safeway
4	B&Q

tblManager
ManagerID (Primary Key)
StoreID (Foreign Key - tblStore)

ManagerName

tblManager

ManagerID	StoreID	ManagerName
1	1	John Smith
2	1	Lee Thomas
3	1	Alison Jones
4	2	Tim O'Brian
5	2	Simon Marsh
6	3	Harry Hill
7	3	Sally Lees
8	4	Jenny Parker
9	4	Ian Jennings
10	4	Fred Lee
11	4	Bill Hardy
12	4	Alan Parker

It also has a Microsoft Access form with two combo boxes.

Figure 1.2.37 Combo boxes

By using Expression builder, the following data is provided:

cboStore
RecordSource: SELECT [tblStore].[lngStoreID], [tblStore].[strStoreName] FROM tblStore;

cboManager
RecordSource: SELECT [tblManager].[lngManagerID], [tblManager].[lngStoreID], [tblManager].
[strManagerName] FROM tblManager;

After this you only want visible those managers that are in the store that has been selected from cboStore.

To only show the managers that are in the store selected from the first combo box, the following code needs adding to the **AfterUpdate** event of **cboStore**:

```
Private Sub cboStore_AfterUpdate()
  Dim sManagerSource As String

  sManagerSource = "SELECT [tblManager].[lngManagerID], " & _
    " [tblManager].[lngStoreID], " & _
    " [tblManager].[strManagerName] " & _
    "FROM tblManager " & _
    "WHERE [lngStoreID] = " & Me.cboStore.Value
  Me.cboManager.RowSource = sManagerSource
  Me.cboManager.Requery
End Sub
```

From this, once a store has been chosen, the list available in combo box 2 will be limited by the choice from the first combo box. Compare the examples shown here, before and after a filter has been set up.

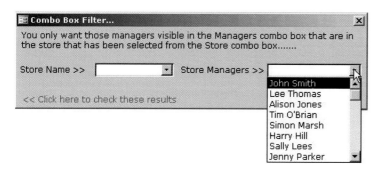

Figure 1.2.38 No filtering done

Once a store is chosen, the list of managers should become restricted to only those that work for that store, as shown in Figure 1.2.39.

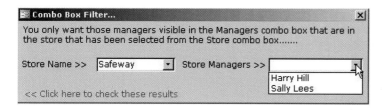

Figure 1.2.39 With filter

Passing multiple parameters to a form

You can use the OpenArgs method to pass one or more parameters from one form to another one. In the following example form, there are two subforms embedded into the main form. These subforms contain details of Home and Away team players.

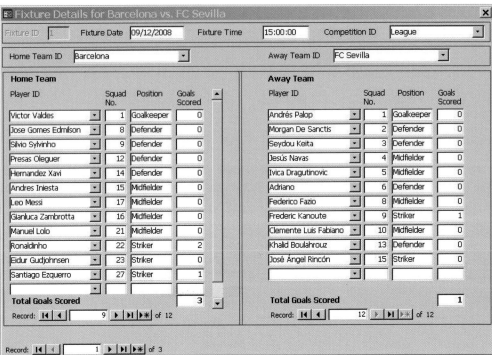

Figure 1.2.40 Fixture results

The combo box list that includes players from the selected teams uses the **NotInList** event procedure (see above), which allows the entry of new player details if they do not have a record in the list.

As the new player details need to be added to a specified team, when the data is assigned, both the player's name and team need to be added.

This action is performed by opening the Player form and populating the Team ID and the Player name, using the data passed in the **OpenArgs** event.

Figure 1.2.41 Not in list dialog

When the new player name is entered, the Not In List dialog box appears. The code that affects the parameters to be set up is shown here.

```
Private Sub cboAwayPlayerID_NotInList(NewData As String, Response As Integer)

    Dim Result
    Dim Msg As String
    Dim CR As String

    CR = Chr$(13)

    ' Exit this subroutine if the combo box was cleared.
    If NewData = "" Then Exit Sub
    ' Ask the user if he or she wishes to add the new Player.
    Msg = "" & NewData & "' is not in the list. " & CR & CR
    Msg = Msg & "Do you want to add it?"
    If MsgBox(Msg, vbQuestion + vbYesNo) = vbYes Then
        ' If the user chose Yes, start the Players form in data entry
        ' mode as a dialog form, passing the new Player name in
        ' NewData to the OpenForm method's OpenArgs argument.

        DoCmd.OpenForm "frmPlayers", , , , acAdd, acDialog, _
        NewData & ";" & Me.Parent.cboAwayTeamID

    End If

End Sub
```

The DoCmd.OpenForm method opens the specified form and passes the OpenArgs data in the **FormLoad** event associated with the form being opened.

Click 'Yes' to bring up the player entry form which opens with data populated from the passed parameters.

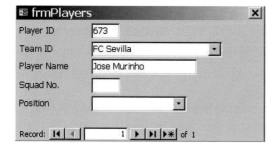

Figure 1.2.42 Player form

The **FormLoad** event uses the following code:

```
Private Sub Form_Load()

' If the form's OpenArgs property has a value, assign the contents
' of OpenArgs to the strPlayerName field. It also sets the new player team name to
' value in main Fixtures form
  Dim strPlayer As String
  Dim lngTeam As Long

  If Not IsNull(Me.OpenArgs) Then
  ' Split OpenArgs data into separate fields
    strPlayer = Left(OpenArgs, InStr(OpenArgs, ";") - 1)
    lngTeam = Mid(OpenArgs, InStr(OpenArgs, ";") + 1)

    Me![strPlayerName] = strPlayer
    Me.lngTeamID = lngTeam

  End If
End Sub
```

The InStr, Left and Mid functions are used to split the data to pass to the correct fields. We split the data either side of the special character that we used to pass the multiple OpenArgs parameters, which was a semi-colon (;).

Archiving old records

An Access database can get full quite quickly when it is in daily use. After a while there may be many records that are not relevant to everyday processing. It is quite normal for businesses to want to keep hold of 'old' data, but keeping this unused data in the current data tables is simply inefficient – hence the need to archive old data away from the processed data.

This is done by transferring the old data from the current file to an archive store and then deleting it from the current file. In other words, by using an Append query, followed by a Delete query.

These can be set up using the interface and run manually, but the most efficient way is to have an archive command button that combines the two functions and does it in one process. An example is shown below which can be adapted to any situation. It should be placed in the on-click event of the button, or could be attached so that it is run on opening the database, or opening a particular form.

Here is the code required to run the process from a command button placed on a form.

```
Private Sub cmdArchiveData_Click()
'Run Archive - Append and Delete

  Dim strSQLAppend As String
  Dim strSQLDelete As String
  Dim errLoop As Error
  Dim dteExpiry As Date

  ' sets to archive any record where date enrolled is over 2 years old
  dteExpiry = DateAdd("yyyy", -2, Date)

  ' Define two SQL statements for action queries.

  strSQLAppend = "INSERT INTO tblExpiredStudents " & _
    "( strStudentID, strFirstName, strLastName, strAddress1, " & _
    "strAddress2, strCity, strCounty, strPostCode, strTelephone, " & _
    "[hypE-mailAddress], dtmDOB, dtmEnrolled, strCourseID ) " & _
    "SELECT tblStudentInformation.strStudentID, " & _
    "tblStudentInformation.strFirstName, " & _
    "tblStudentInformation.strLastName, " & _
    "tblStudentInformation.strAddress1, " & _
    "tblStudentInformation.strAddress2, " & _
    "tblStudentInformation.strCity, " & _
    "tblStudentInformation.strCounty, " & _
    "tblStudentInformation.strPostCode, " & _
    "tblStudentInformation.strTelephone, " & _
    "tblStudentInformation.[hypE-mailAddress], " & _
    "tblStudentInformation.dtmDOB, " & _
    "tblStudentInformation.dtmEnrolled, " & _
    "tblStudentInformation.strCourseID " & _
    "FROM tblStudentInformation " & _
    "WHERE tblStudentInformation.dtmEnrolled <= #" & dteExpiry & "#;"

  strSQLDelete = "DELETE tblStudentInformation.strStudentID, " & _
    "tblStudentInformation.strFirstName, " & _
    "tblStudentInformation.strLastName, " & _
    "tblStudentInformation.strAddress1, " & _
    "tblStudentInformation.strAddress2, " & _
    "tblStudentInformation.strCity, " & _
    "tblStudentInformation.strCounty, " & _
    "tblStudentInformation.strPostCode, " & _
    "tblStudentInformation.strTelephone, " & _
    "tblStudentInformation.[hypE-mailAddress], " & _
    "tblStudentInformation.dtmDOB, " & _
    "tblStudentInformation.dtmEnrolled, " & _
    "tblStudentInformation.strCourseID " & _
    "FROM tblStudentInformation " & _
    "WHERE tblStudentInformation.dtmEnrolled <= #" & dteExpiry & "#;"

End Sub
```

Non-standard report groupings

Reports can be grouped on any field (e.g. Department Name), including numeric fields. However, when numeric fields are found by the report wizard it offers further choices for grouping, as shown below.

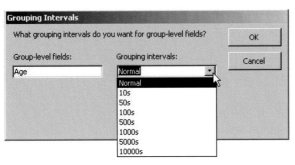

Figure 1.2.43 Numeric groupings

However, if different groupings are required, then a function will have to be written and added to the database and an extra field added to the query upon which the report is designed.

For example, we could group the data by age ranges – 0–17, 18–25, 26–30, 31–35, etc. – using a database based upon Employees. In the Employee table one of the fields would be the Employee Date Of Birth. This information would be used to calculate the Age value, but also as a field that includes the data that we are going to group on.

The created function uses a DateDiff calculation to calculate the Age, and also includes a SELECT CASE statement that will create the Age Group Ranges.

```
Public Function AgeGroup(dtmBirthDate As Date) As String

  Dim intAge As Integer

  'Age Calculation
  intAge = DateDiff("yyyy", [dtmBirthDate], Now()) + _
    Int(Format(Now(), "mmdd") < Format([dtmBirthDate], "mmdd"))

  Select Case intAge

    'For each Age range, write out Age Group (used in qry)
  Case 0 To 17
    AgeGroup = "0-17"
  Case 18 To 25
    AgeGroup = "18-25"
  Case 26 To 30
    AgeGroup = "26-30"
  Case 31 To 35
    AgeGroup = "31-35"
  Case 36 To 40
    AgeGroup = "36-40"
  Case 41 To 45
    AgeGroup = "41-45"
  Case 45 to 50
    AgeGroup = "46-50"
  Case is > 50
    AgeGroup = "50+"
  End Select

End Function
```

Once the function has been written, the query will need two extra fields added to it, one so that it is able to show 'Age' on the report (using the DateDiff function, as used in the above function) and the other to show the grouping.

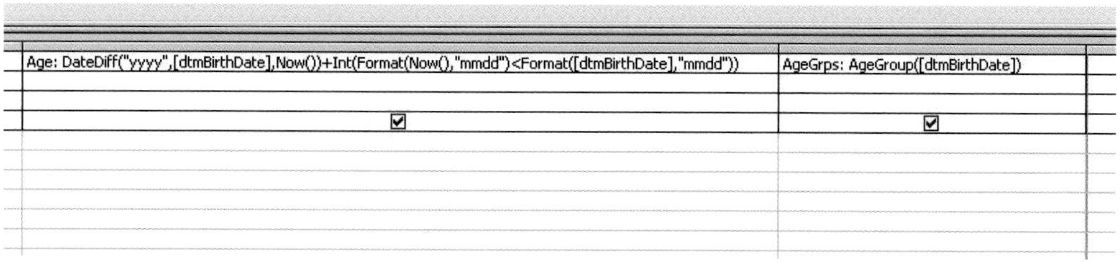

Age: DateDiff("yyyy",[dtmBirthDate],Now())+Int(Format(Now(),"mmdd")<Format([dtmBirthDate],"mmdd"))	AgeGrps: AgeGroup([dtmBirthDate])	
☑	☑	

Figure 1.2.44 Query fields

Normal report wizard report setup will then produce the report grouped as required.

Employee Age Groups

Age Groups	Age	First Name	Last Name	Birth Date
0-17	17	Oliver	Timbury	06-Apr-90
18-25	18	Tina	Smythe	29-Jun-89
	22	Niele	Lessing	20-Sep-85
26-30	28	Gary	Richardson	15-Nov-79
31-35	33	Samuel	Jackson	14-Aug-74
36-40	38	Gail	James	08-Nov-69
41-45	41	Anne	Brewster	27-Jan-66
	44	Michael	Sullivan	02-Jul-63
	44	Janet	Levell	30-Aug-63
46-50	47	Robert	Melling	29-May-60
	49	Laura	Callaghan	09-Jan-58
50+	52	Steven	Baxter	04-Mar-55
	55	Andrew	Foster	19-Feb-52
	58	Nancy	Smythe	08-Dec-49
	70	Margaret	Porter	19-Sep-37

Figure 1.2.45 Grouped report

1.2.5 Desktop publishing

There are numerous specialist desktop publishing packages available – Pagemaker, InDesign and QuarkExpress are just some of the commercially used packages used by graphic designers.

For AS-level students, and the majority of non-professional graphic designers, the functions found in Microsoft Publisher are usually more than sufficient for the majority of requirements. Even Microsoft Word has many facilities that emulate a desktop publisher program – for example, the ability to combine graphics and images with text, tables and columns. The quality of text and page formatting options in MS Word are comparable with any desktop publishing package of 15 years ago.

The functions within MS Publisher are similar across the different versions but MS Publisher 2007 has enhanced Mail Merge, Catalogue Merge, and new E-Mail Merge to create personalised publications for print or email distribution. Merge task pane options guide the user through the process of selecting lists, adding text and image fields with bookmarks and personalised hyperlinks, or previewing and completing a mailing. Improvements in email distribution and viewing, including support for sending multi-page publications as a single page message, make it easier than ever to create and send publications as email messages.

Connecting text frames

If there is too much text for the text box, then normally the excess text will 'disappear' into the overflow area, where it cannot be seen. A pop-up box will offer to flow the text into another available text box, if one exists. This may or may not be where you wish the text to go, so it is better to control it yourself. Ensure that the Connect Text Frames toolbar is available by clicking on **View** > **Toolbars** > **Connect Text Frames**. While on the overflowing frame, choose the connect frame option to send the text to the frame you want. A whole set of frames can be connected in the order desired by repeating the above instruction. A small forward and backward icon appears on any active box indicating that it is part of a 'story' and is connected to other frames.

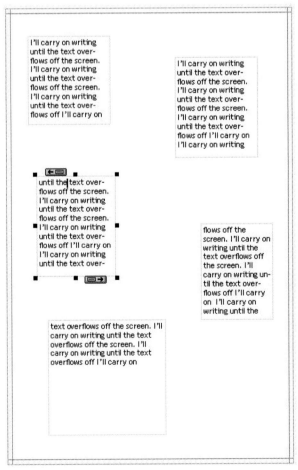

Figure 1.2.46 Text Frame flow

Object layering

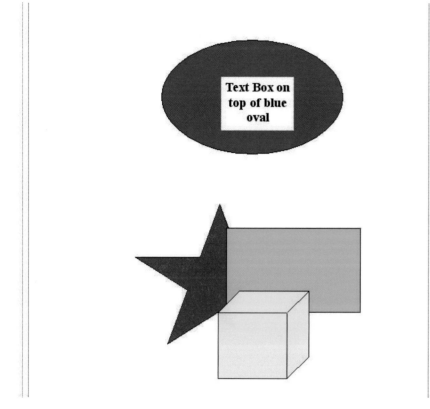

Figure 1.2.47 Layered objects

Any object (text frame, picture frame, shape or symbol, etc.) can be laid on top of another and there are various ways of manipulating the individual elements or the whole group.

For example, in the image above, where a text box has been laid over a coloured shape, it is obvious the text box is separate to the shape. By formatting the text box to be transparent, it looks as though the text is part of the oval.

Figure 1.2.48 Amended objects

On the image below, the order of the layered shapes can be changed by highlighting the layer required to be moved and choosing an action from the **Arrange** menu. Click **Arrange** > **Order** to move the layers forwards or backwards – **Send to Front** takes the layer to the very top of the object pile whereas **Send Forwards** moves it forward one layer at a time.

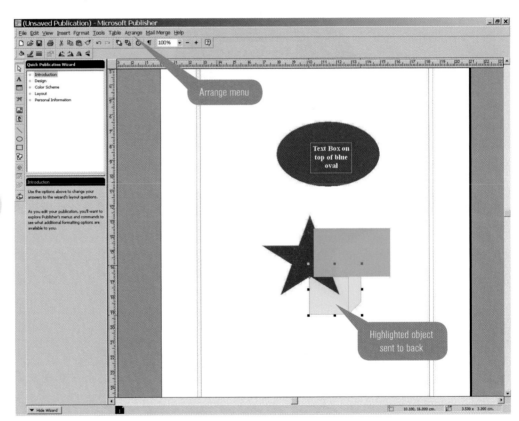

Figure 1.2.49 Amended objects

1.2.6 Presentation software

Producing a presentation is quite simple using the software packages that are available. Examples below are using Microsoft PowerPoint 2007, although most of these functions also appear in previous versions and most other presentation software.

Again, it is assumed that an AS-level student already knows how to produce a presentation with different slide layouts, incorporating images and charts, and has also explored and used slide transitions and animations.

Creating a Custom Slide Show

The following shows you how to make the most efficient use of a full presentation of slides. If communicating the same message to different audiences it's likely that certain slides will not be relevant to all audiences, but by creating custom slide shows, the same set of slides can be used for all audiences.

When your presentation slides are all complete, on the **Slide Show** ribbon, click the arrow next to **Custom Slide Shows** in the **Start Slide Show** group, then click on **Custom Show**. Choose the **New** button and a **Define Custom Show** dialog box will appear. Click on the slides required for this particular run-through and add them to the show. Repeat for other custom shows from the same set of slides.

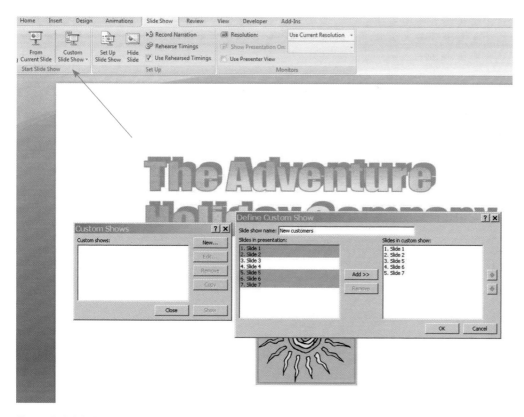

Figure 1.2.50 Defining a Custom Slide Show

The order of the slides can be changed at any time, either at creation or later on, by clicking on **Edit** and using the arrow keys on the right hand side of the dialog box. To run a custom show, click the arrow next to **Custom Slide Show** and the different show titles will be shown, click on the one you want to run.

Features that can be included in a presentation

- **Hyperlinks** can be used which allow the user to jump to:

  - certain slides within the presentation as would be the case in a custom show;

  - different presentations entirely;

  - Microsoft Office Word documents;

  - Microsoft Office Excel worksheets;

  - locations on the Internet or an intranet;

  - or email addresses.

  Hyperlinks can be created from any object, including text, shapes, tables, graphs, and pictures. The **Hyperlink** function is found in the **Links** group on the **Insert** ribbon and the dialog box shown in Figure 1.2.51 offers different options.

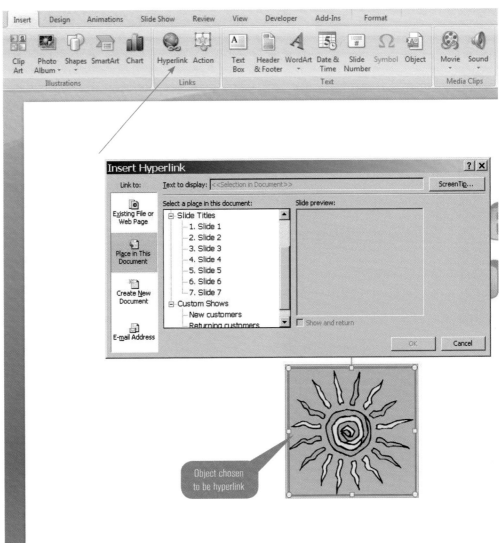

Figure 1.2.51 Hyperlinks

■ **Action** buttons are predefined symbols that can be added to a presentation and used to launch hyperlinks. Action buttons contain shapes, such as right and left arrows. Use them when commonly understood symbols for going to the next, previous, first, and last slides are required. PowerPoint also has action buttons for playing movies or sounds. Action buttons can be found in the **Links** group on the **Insert** ribbon. The following dialog box appears, offering options for what happens on button click or mouse over.

Figure 1.2.52 Action buttons

■ Add narration to make the presentation accessible for sight-impaired users. On the **Slide Show** menu, narration can be added to the presentation at the time of creation, or added later. When narration is added to a slide, a sound icon appears on the slide. As with any sound, you can either click the icon to play the sound or set the sound to play automatically. Voice narration takes precedence over other sounds, and only one sound can play at a time in a presentation. As a result, other sounds that are set to play automatically in a presentation are overridden by a narration and will not play. However, sounds that are set to play when clicked will still play when you click them. As the narration is being recorded, the software automatically records the time spent on each slide and offers these slide timings for you to save, if required. The narration can be linked, in a separate sound file, or embedded within the presentation. The **Package for CD** feature should be used for distributing the presentation. Later editing can be done using sound file editing software.

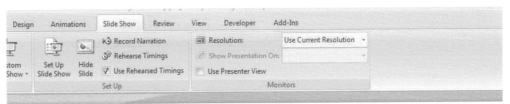

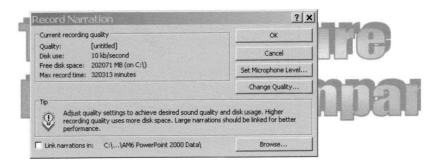

Figure 1.2.53 Narration

■ **Rehearse Timings** is a feature used when there is no recorded narration and you would like to test the time taken by an average person to read the information on a slide. The feature, accessed from the **Slide Show** menu, is straightforward to use and gives you the opportunity to amend and refine the timings until you are happy with them.

■ **Set up the presentation to run at a kiosk** is used to produce a self-running presentation. There may well be a requirement that the presentation produced is to be on permanent display, in a kiosk at an information centre, for instance. There are various methods of ensuring the successful self-running of a presentation in PowerPoint 2007.

This is the point where decisions about the presentation's actions are made. On the **Slide Show** menu, choose the **Set Up Slide Show** button to bring up a dialog box that gives options about the performance of the presentation. The show must have automatic timings, navigation hyperlinks or action buttons; otherwise it will not advance beyond the first slide.

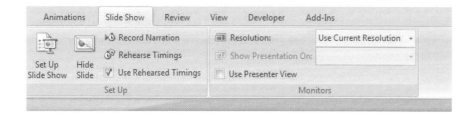

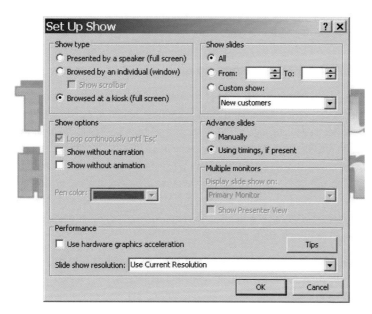

Figure 1.2.54 Kiosk

There are some other useful features and functions within MS PowerPoint 2007 and they are further explained in the multimedia section below.

1.2.7 Web development software

Websites can be developed using simple HTML (Hyper Text Mark-up Language) statements in Notepad or any simple HTML editor. HTML codes are used to define styles for the required text and images. Frames, tables, thumbnails and hyperlinks can easily be created with this method of web page creation. It is simple and most pages designed using this method work with ease. The developer has full control over what is being displayed, or how the buttons will work, but the process is long and painstaking and it is easy to forget a closing control code, which can have unexpected effects.

Many generic WYSIWYG (What You See Is What You Get) style packages also have facilities for saving something designed within them as a web page. Microsoft products, such as MS Word, MS Publisher and MS PowerPoint, have such features. Choose File > Save as > Other formats (in 2007) and choose one of the web page options. Some HTML editors also work in WYSIWYG mode – a simple search engine request will find a selection of these, some free to download.

However, there are a number of specific software packages designed for producing websites with multimedia add-ins. Adobe's Creative Suite 3 (CS3), formerly Macromedia Studio 8, contains a range of tools specifically designed for website development. Dreamweaver, Flash and Fireworks are used extensively in the commercial arena for building websites.

The following are just two ways to make your websites more professional-looking using some of the Dreamweaver functionality.

Creating a website using a cascading style sheet in Dreamweaver

Cascading style sheets (CSS) are a collection of formatting rules that control the appearance of content in a web page. Using CSS styles to format a page separates content from presentation. The content of the page – the HTML code – resides in the HTML file, and the CSS rules defining the presentation of the code reside in another file (an external style sheet) or in another part of the HTML document (usually the head section). Separating content from presentation makes it much easier to maintain the appearance of the site from a central location because you don't need to update every property on every page whenever you want to make a change. It also results in a simpler and cleaner HTML code, which provides shorter browser loading times, and simplifies navigation for people with accessibility issues (for example, those using screen readers).

CSS gives you great flexibility and control over the exact appearance of your page. With CSS you can control many text properties including specific fonts and font sizes; bold, italics, underlining and text shadows; text colour and background colour; link colour and link underlining; and much more. By using CSS to control your fonts, you can also ensure a more consistent treatment of your page layout and appearance in multiple browsers. In addition to text formatting, you can use CSS to control the format and positioning of block-level elements in a web page. A block-level element is a stand-alone piece of content, usually separated by a new line in the HTML, and visually formatted as a block. For example, <h1> tags, <p> tags and <div> tags all produce block-level elements on a web page. You can set margins and borders for block-level elements, position them in a specific location, add background colour to them, float text around them, and so on. Manipulating block-level elements is, in essence, the way you lay out pages with CSS.

Open an existing html file and click the CSS button in the Properties panel at the bottom of the window to open the CSS panel.

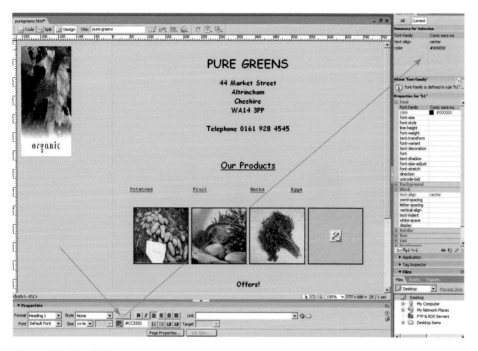

Figure 1.2.55 CSS panel

We're going to look at how to create new rules with CSS that can then be applied across many different text blocks. The following shows how we can make changes to the rules or tags that have been applied to the screen shown above.

■ The cursor is placed on the <h1> tag, which is the heading 'PURE GREENS', so the associated properties for that tag are shown and can be amended.

■ Amendments to the font are made and the item changes. The same is done for the other tags on this page (<h2> (the address) and <h3> (Our Products)).

■ These changes are shown immediately so you can preview and amend the effect if necessary.

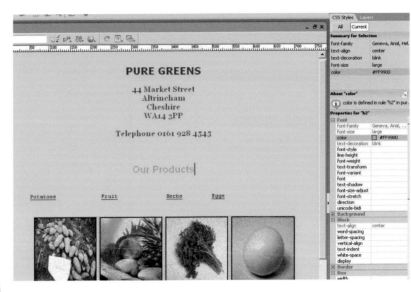

Figure 1.2.56 CSS changes

Creating a new rule

1   Place the insertion point in the document, and then do one of the following to open the **New CSS Rule** dialog box:

■   Select **Text** > **CSS Styles** > **New**

Or

■   In the **CSS Styles** panel (**Window** > **CSS Styles**), click the **New CSS Rule** (+) button located in the lower-right side of the panel.

Figure 1.2.57 Creating a new CSS rule

2   Define the type of CSS style you want to create.

■ To create a custom style that can be applied as a class attribute to a range or block of text, select the **Class** option and then enter a name for the style in the **Name text** box.

■ To redefine the default formatting of a specific HTML tag, select the **Tag** option and then enter an HTML tag in the **Tag text** box or select one from the pop-up menu.

■ To define the formatting for a particular combination of tags or for all tags that contain a specific ID attribute, select the **Advanced** option and then type in one or more HTML tags in the **Selector text** box or select one from the drop-down menu. The selectors (known as pseudo-class selectors) available from the drop-down menu are a:active, a:hover, a:link, and a:visited.

3   Select the location in which the style will be defined, and then click **OK**.

■ To place the style in a style sheet that is already attached to the document, select the style sheet.

■ To create an external style sheet, select **New Style Sheet File**.

■ To embed the style in the current document, select **This Document Only**.

4   In the **CSS Rule Definition** dialog box, select the style options you want to set for the new CSS rule.

Class names must begin with a period and can contain any combination of letters and numbers (for example, .myhead1). If you don't enter a beginning period, Dreamweaver automatically enters it for you.

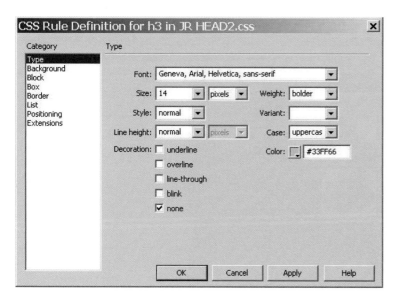

Figure 1.2.58 Define the rule

5   When you are finished setting style properties, click **OK**.

To use an external style sheet on another html file, attach the CSS style sheet by opening **Text** > **CSS styles** > **Attach CSS style sheet**, then enter the name of the file containing the style sheet.

There are many ways to format a website using CSS. One thing to remember is that the 'cascade' in the term is to indicate that there are various levels of style override. Some web browsers have their own style, for instance Internet Explorer displays most body text in Times New Roman, size Medium, as a default.

Theoretically, any specific style sheet that is attached to an uploaded website takes precedence, but be warned: do look out for changes to your designs due to this aspect of web page creation. You may find that the page displays differently in different web browsers, and this is an aspect that should be tested before publishing a website.

Using frames

Frames are used on a web page to control the content and to improve the appearance. Each page's frame has its own HTML file.

Here is a website front page with two frames. The information panel on the left hand side is INFO.HTM and the large frame on the right is called MAIN.HTM.

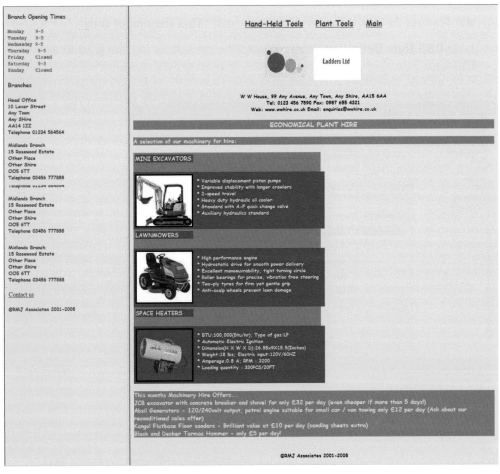

Figure 1.2.59 Framed window

It is easy to edit the page as a whole frameset, as you can see what is happening as you go along. Creating new frames is done by **Insert** > **HTML** > **Frames**, and choosing where you want to position the new frame. Then text and other objects can be placed at will in the normal way.

Figure 1.2.60 Frame added top left

Each new frame must be saved so that the overall frameset can be saved. Use **File** > **Save Frameset As** for individual frames, then **File** > **Save All** for the whole frameset. Only when the frameset is saved will the whole page behave as one.

1.2.8 Multimedia software

Most generic software packages have the ability to insert various multimedia files within documents, in spreadsheets and on websites. For example, you can add images, both still and moving, and sounds to an MS PowerPoint presentation, and packages like Dreamweaver have Insert Media functions that allow all sorts of sound and image files to be included.

MS PowerPoint has a **Create Photo Album** function which can be found in the **Illustrations** group on the **Insert** ribbon. Use the arrow by **Photo Album** to reveal a drop-down menu to see the options to create or edit albums.

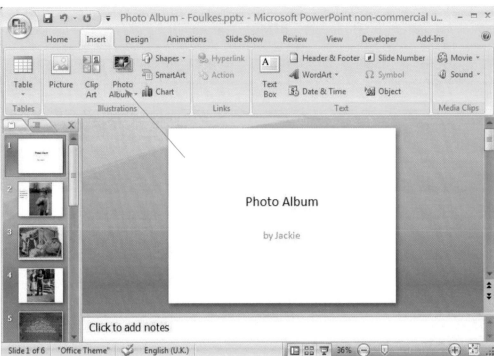

Figure 1.2.61 Photo Album

A dialog box pops up so the user can pick pictures to add to the album. They can be sorted into an order at any time, and text and sound, etc. can be added as for any other presentation.

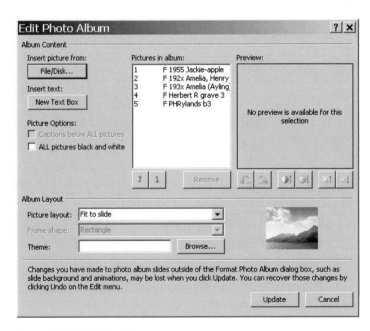

Figure 1.2.62 Pick pictures

However, there is also a multitude of software available for creating multimedia elements and the program Magic Morph is used in this section. Use a search engine to find a copy of the software to download.Magic Morph allows you to create an .AVI, .GIF or .SWF animation by changing one picture into another. Further examples of how to manipulate still and moving images and sounds will be looked at in the next sections.

The first step is to load up a source image and a target image. Press **OK** and three panels appear, one of the source image, one of the target image and one that is titled the Morph Image, a mixture of the two.

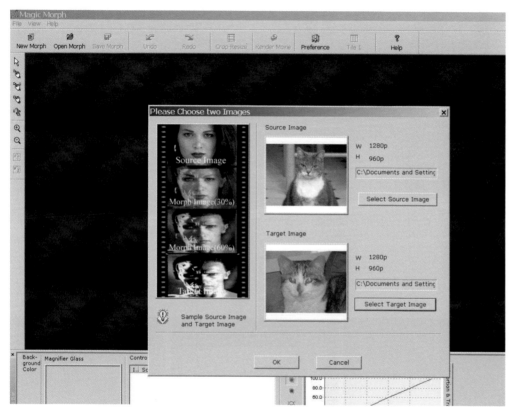

Figure 1.2.63 Morph, Choose images

Use the selection tools on the left hand side to add control points to both source and target images in turn. There should be as many control points as possible; the more there are, the slower the morph. As an example, points could be at the end of each eye, two or three points on each ear, nose, contours of the face and body and so on.

The magnifier area at the bottom left of the screen allows precision to match the control points.

Figure 1.2.64 Control points matching

Once all control points have been added you can see that the coordinates have been recorded in the central display box at the bottom of the screen.

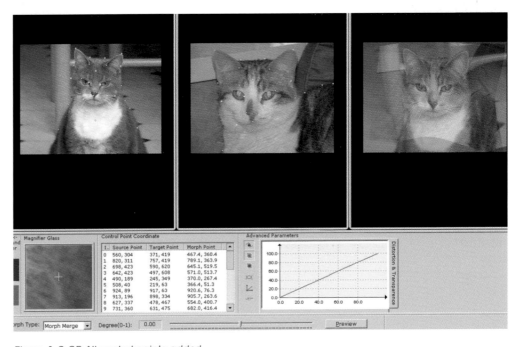

Figure 1.2.65 All control points added

Once you have deselected all of the control point tools, the **Preview** bar can be used to see the effect before saving your work.

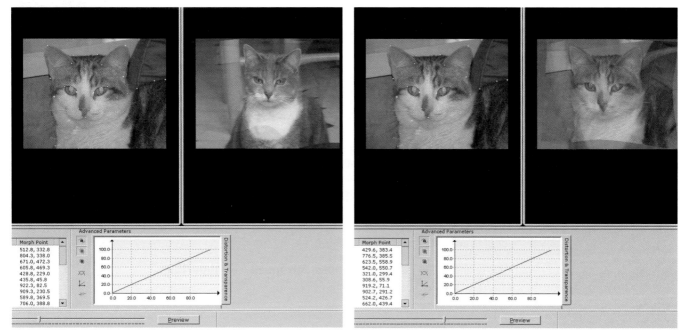

Figure 1.2.66 At .25 morphed   Figure 1.2.67 At .75 morphed

Finally, choose the **Render Movie** button to create the file required. Look at the number of frames and number of frames per second and adjust these to decide the length of the clip – the default is 30 frames and 25 FPS – too quick for most viewers to register! This file can now be used to import into whichever application you desire.

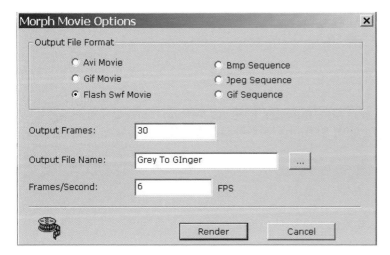

Figure 1.2.68 Save as movie

1.2.9 Sound manipulation software

Creating a simple Podcast

The Podcast is created in the free software package Audacity and the following demonstration is an example of the features which are most likely to be useful. After completing this section you will be able to produce an MP3 track that combines backing music and your own vocals.

Type Audacity into a search engine and you will be offered the option to download it. It is also necessary to download the free MP3 encoder called Limp before starting. Finally, some music is required, which could be stored on the school network or, if you are doing this at home, you may have CD tracks stored in iTunes. If you don't have iTunes, this software can also be downloaded free-of-charge. In addition to a computer system, the hardware required is a headset with microphone so that you can capture and listen to audio sound.

Importing tracks

The first task is to convert the sound file using iTunes into a file that is accepted by Audacity. You will need to convert the file into an AIFF file.

Open iTunes, go to **Edit**, **Preferences**, **Advanced** then **Importing**.

Figure 1.2.69 Converting the track to be accepted by Audacity

Use the drop-down menu to select **AIFF Encoder**. Under the **Setting** drop-down menu select **Custom** and click on **Use Default Settings** followed by **OK** and **OK** again.

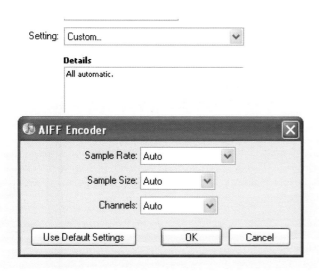

Figure 1.2.70 Defining the settings for converting

Right click on the track to be edited in Audacity and select **Convert Selection to AIFF**.

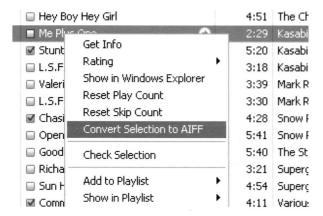

Figure 1.2.71 Specifying the track to convert

Close iTunes and open Audacity. To import the recently converted file, go to **Project** then **Import Audio**.

Figure 1.2.72 Importing the converted track

Navigate to the converted file and select it. Only a few seconds are required to import the track. You may find that there are two versions of the track you want. To make it easier to find and import the AIFF file, change the file type of AIFF files.

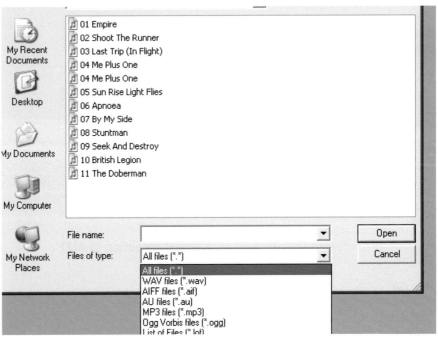

Figure 1.2.73 Locating AIFF files

This will only show the files that Audacity will accept.

Figure 1.2.74 Displaying AIFF files

Select the file you want and click on **Open**. The audio will be displayed like the image below and can now be edited.

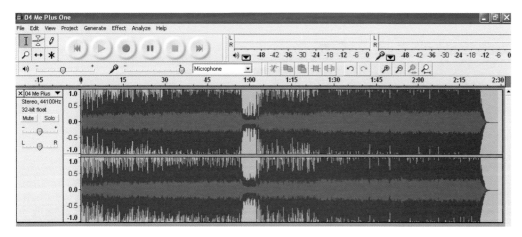

Figure 1.2.75 Track displayed ready for editing

Editing tracks

While a track is playing it cannot be edited. It is important to remember to stop it, select the area to edit then choose the desired edit. The **Select** tool is one of the most useful at this stage.

In order to reduce the length of the track or remove sections that are not required, simply highlight and cut sections out. By placing the cursor at the start of the section to be cut out and dragging to the right, the area to be cut is highlighted. Then use the **Cut** icon.

Figure 1.2.76 Locating the select tool

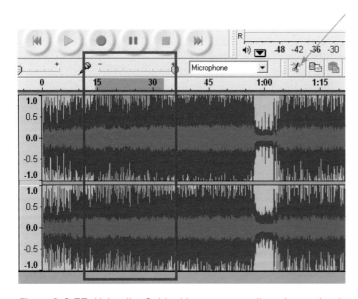

Figure 1.2.77 Using the Cut tool to remove sections from a track

To improve the accuracy of the cut, use the **Zoom** tool to zoom in on the digital sound wave and show smaller frames of time. Editing is performed in exactly the same way as this.

Figure 1.2.78 *The zoom tool allows a user to identify small time frames for editing*

The track is shown in greater detail the further you zoom.

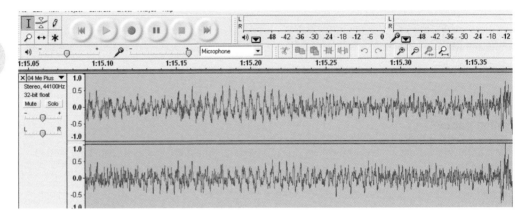

Figure 1.2.79 *An example of a track that has been zoomed into*

You may want to see a lot of detail if you need to reduce the audio by a certain length of time, for example, when it is to be used on a film which is shorter than the length of the track, or create several small sections of a number of tracks to be layered into one film.

Adding personal audio

When the backing track is ready, personal audio can be added. Go to **Project** > **New Audio Track**.

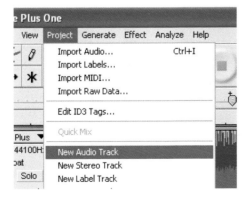

Figure 1.2.80 *Preparing to add personal audio*

Position the mouse on the timeline showing the backing track where you want the recorded audio to go, click **Record** and start speaking.

You will see sound lines move across the screen if the vocals are being captured. When you have finished talking, click the **Stop** button.

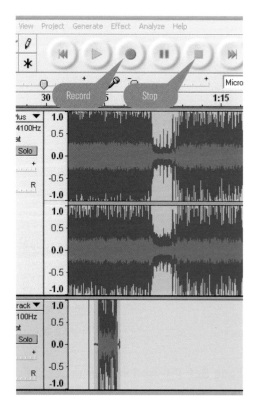

Figure 1.2.81 Using the Record and Stop buttons to capture spoken audio

It is possible to work on both soundtracks independently until you are happy with them. The **Time Shift** tool also allows the user to pick up the recorded music or verbal data and move it to another position along the timeline.

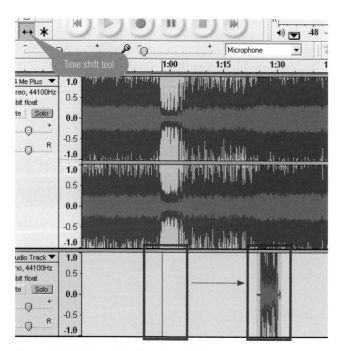

Figure 1.2.82 Locating the Time shift tool

When the **Play** button is pushed, both tracks can be heard at the same time. To listen to just one, click the **Mute** button on the track you don't want to hear (Figure 1.2.83).

Figure 1.2.83 Applying the Mute option

Using Fade or Silence features

If there is a need to reduce the volume on the backing track so that verbal data can be heard over it with more clarity, the **Fade** tool can be used.

Select the area which is to be faded and use **Effect** > **Fade Out**. The sound wave will be altered on the screen.

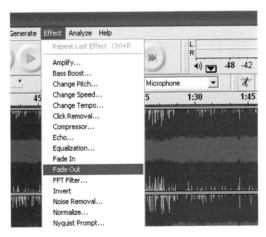

Figure 1.2.84 The Effect menu gives lots of options that can be experimented with

If the fade feature is not good enough you can use the silence features. Select the area to silence and click on the **Silence Selection** tool.

If you then decide you preferred the faded version after all, you can use the **Undo** tool to reverse your actions. It's a useful tool in this package as there is likely to be a lot of experimentation during editing.

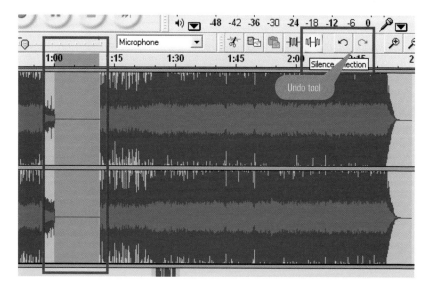

Figure 1.2.85 Use the Undo tool in situations where the previous edit is not satisfactory

Saving as an MP3 file for podcasting

This is the final stage and will only work if the Limp MP3 encoder software has been downloaded. It will download as a zipped file. Extract all the files and then leave it alone.

Go back to the file in Audacity containing the prepared audio. You will now need to edit the ID3 tags. This can be done before saving by going to **Project** > **Edit ID3 Tags** (Figure 1.2.86).

You will need to fill out the fields in the dialog box as shown in Figure 1.2.87 and click **OK**.

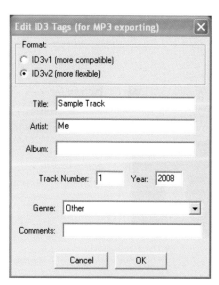

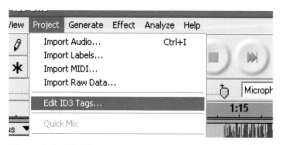

Figure 1.2.86 Use the Project menu to edit the ID3 Tags

Figure 1.2.87 The ID3 Tags dialog box

To save go to **File** > **Export as MP3**.

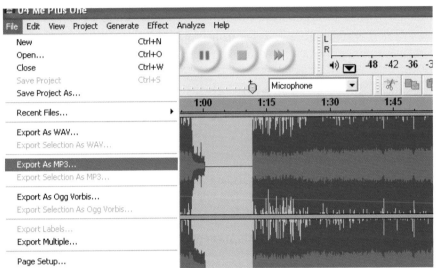

Figure 1.2.88 The file needs to be exported into MP3 format

The first time you do this you will be directed to navigate to Limp MP3 encoder. Follow the instructions and run the file through Limp.

The dialog box in Figure 1.2.89 should appear after you have decided where to save the file.

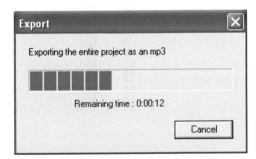

Figure 1.2.89 Exporting the file

The end result is a homemade MP3 file which can be added to a movie or played on an iPod as a podcast. Open iTunes and test it out.

Figure 1.2.90 The finished track represented as an icon

1.2.10 Video manipulation software

Creating a movie

Movies, short films or adverts are an excellent way to convey messages without using masses of text. They provide the opportunity to mix together motion, sound and narration to give an all-round package that helps to convey information.

This section will show you how to transfer data from a DV video camera right through to producing a complete file which can be burnt onto a DVD or played on a computer. The software used is Windows Movie Maker.

Transferring data

After capturing the data on your video camera, plug in the Firewire cable, which connects from the DV slot in the camera, to an available port in the computer. The camera should be set to play.

Open the software Windows Movie Maker and the following screen will appear.

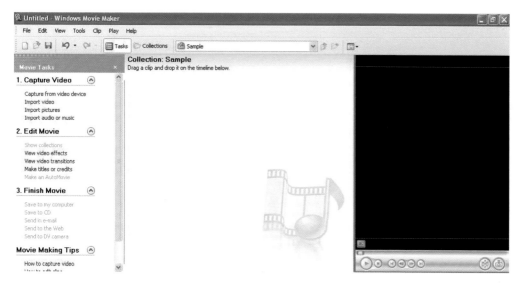

Figure 1.2.91 The opening screen for Windows Movie Maker

From the left hand side, select **Capture from video device**.

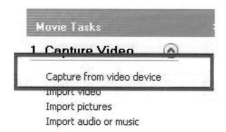

Figure 1.2.92 The initial stage of capturing video footage

Next give the project a meaningful title and make sure it is saved in a folder you can navigate back to later. Then click on **Next**.

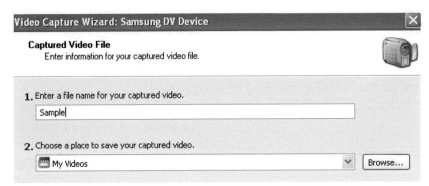

Figure 1.2.93 Using a sensible a meaningful name will enable you to locate the file at a later date

When presented with the following screen, select the option most appropriate for your project.

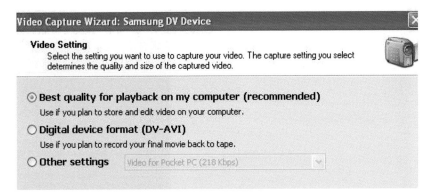

Figure 1.2.94 Selecting the quality of copy required will depend on available disk space and intended audience or purpose of the film

The next screen asks if you want to capture the data on the whole tape, or just a section. For this sample, which is quite short, it is only necessary to capture parts of the tape manually.

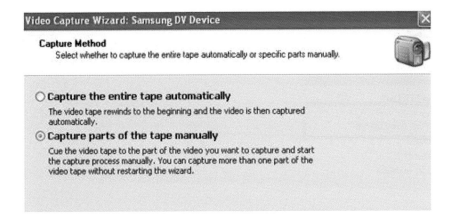

Figure 1.2.95 Defining the capture method

This screen allows you to set the recording at the point where the capture needs to start.

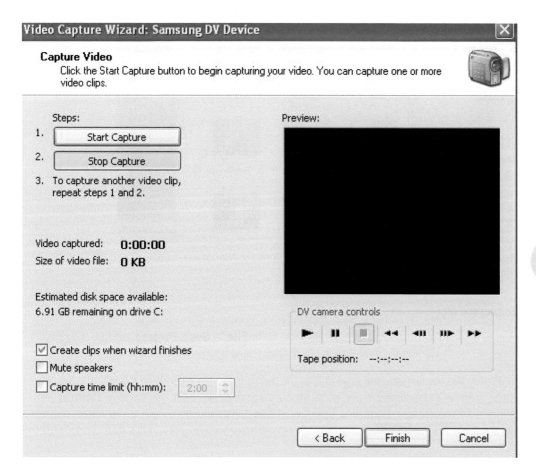

Figure 1.2.96 The Video Capture dialog box with the options required to specify the footage required

Use the **DV camera control** tools (Figure 1.2.97) to line up the tape then click **Start Capture**. When the amount of data required has been captured, press **Stop Capture** (Figure 1.2.98).

Figure 1.2.97 The DV camera controls

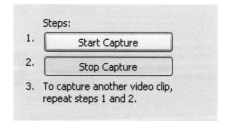

Figure 1.2.98 The Start Capture and Stop Capture buttons

When the data is captured, the movie is broken up into sections.

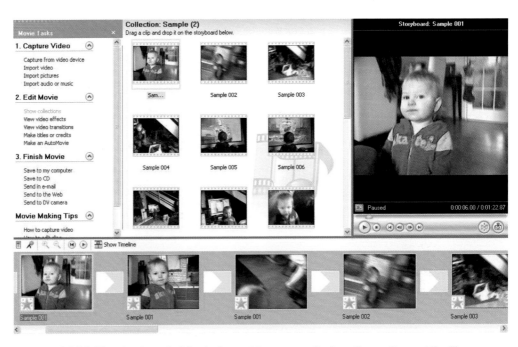

Figure 1.2.99 The screen displays snap shots from the start of each section from the footage

Editing the film

Prior to editing it is a good idea to save the work. Go to **File** > **Save Project** and give it a sensible file name, and save it in the location where you wish to find it later.

In order to edit the film, you will need to drag the panels in the top onto the storyboard (the bottom pane). To move all the panels in one go, position the cursor between the panels, press **Control** and **A** together (the keyboard shortcut for selecting all items), then use the mouse to drag them all to the storyboard.

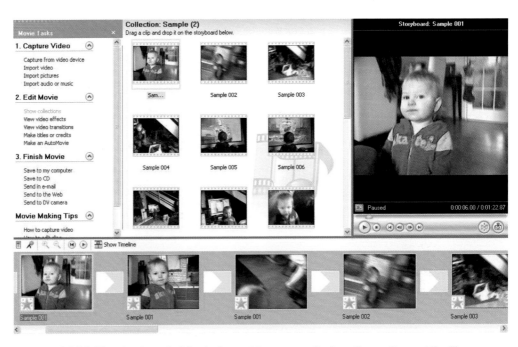

Figure 1.2.100 The storyboard at the bottom of the screen displays the sections of the film

After watching a sequence, it may be desirable to remove it. This is achieved by using the timeline view.

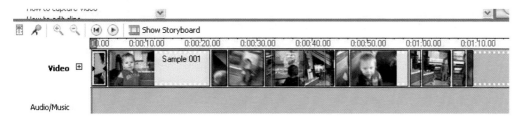

Figure 1.2.101 Use the timeline view to edit sections of the film

Use the **Zoom** tool to make the sections longer and give more detail, making them easier to crop.

Figure 1.2.102 The timeline view increased to give a greater view to a portion of time in the film to be edited

Click on the timeline at the point where you would like to start the cut. Then click on the **Cut** tool, which will chop the film at that point.

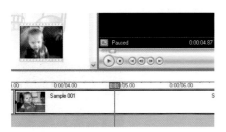

Figure 1.2.103 Selecting the start point where the film is to be cropped

Now position the cursor on the timeline at the end of the cut sequence. Use the **Cut** tool again.

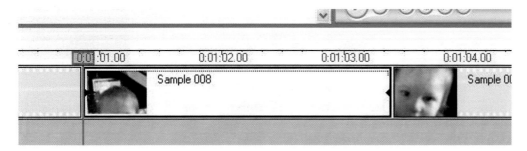

Figure 1.2.104 Selecting the end point of the footage to remove

71

Right click on the newly created section and choose **Delete** from the menu. It will be removed from the film.

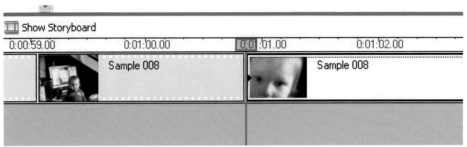

Figure 1.2.105 The footage with the section removed

It will almost always be necessary to remove frames or scenes from the data captured on the camera. The ability to remove unwanted scenes will also save file space later and improve the final film. Using the **Cut** tool enables a long scene to be divided into smaller sections too, where you may need to include other features, like a screen title or slow motion.

Applying transitions

The option of including transitions between scenes reduces the choppy feel of a home movie. It is easy to apply these between scenes or frames where the editor has deliberately placed a cut.

You will need to make sure that the storyboard view is visible to add a transition.

Select **Video Transitions** from the **Edit Movie** menu. Click on the transition you would like to include and drag it in between the scenes to the point where it is to appear.

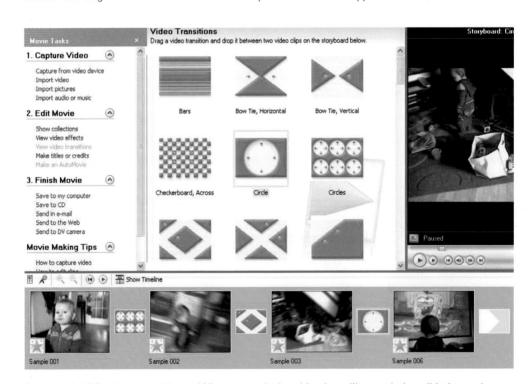

Figure 1.2.106 Video transitions. When you select a video transition and place it between two frames in the storyboard, its symbol will appear in the storyboard

2. Edit Movie

Figure 1.2.107 *The Edit Movie menu*

Figure 1.2.108 *The Circles transition symbol*

Figure 1.2.109 *The storyboard showing the Circles transition in place between the two frames*

It is advisable to experiment with various transitions to see which options work best at various phases of the film. Using too many can make the final production clumsy and unpleasant to view. To see what has been achieved so far, use the video box on the left of the timeline to run the film.

Adding special effects

This is done in a similar way to adding transitions.

Select **View video effects**. Click on the one you want and drag it to the bottom left corner of the scene where it is to be applied.

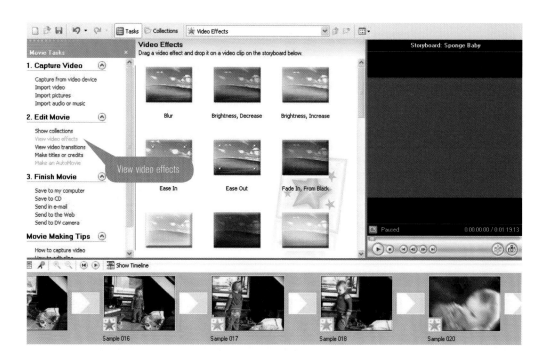

Figure 1.2.110 *Select View video effects from the left-hand menu*

Figure 1.2.111 One of the available options

Figure 1.2.112 Drag the option to the scene where it is to be applied

Figure 1.2.113 Transition is represented on the scene

Movie Tasks

1. Capture Video

Capture from video device
Import video
Import pictures
Import audio or music

Figure 1.2.114 The menu used to import sound affects

Adding music

To bring the movie to life it is possible to add a soundtrack at various stages. The backing music may have already been created in Audacity or it is possible to use a track stored elsewhere. If a track which is stored in iTunes is required, it will have to be converted into AIFF format otherwise it will be rejected by Windows Movie Maker.

Select **Import audio or music** (Figure 1.2.114). Navigate to where the track is stored, select it and click on **Import**.

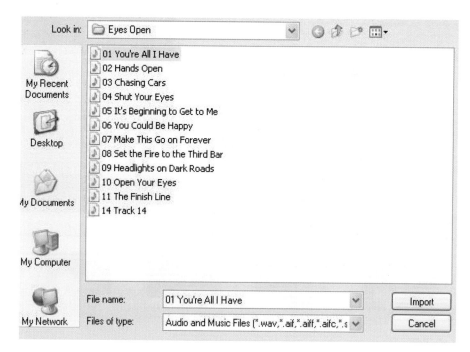

Figure 1.2.115 Locating the desired file

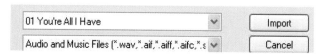

Figure 1.2.116 The selected file is displayed

The soundtrack will appear as a panel with the movie scenes.

Figure 1.2.117 *The selected file is represented as a tile*

In timeline view, drag the audio panel to the audio/music column under the film.

Figure 1.2.118 *Audio file is displayed under the scenes from the film*

Using the **Drag and trim** tool at the edge of the audio music line it is possible to make the track fit the movie.

Figure 1.2.119 *This will reduce the length of the track but will mean losing sections of the original audio*

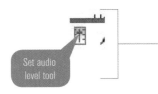

Set audio level tool

To ensure the music does not drown out the original audio in the film use the **Set Audio Level** tool and move the pointer on the toolbar to gain the desired balance between the original audio and the added soundtrack.

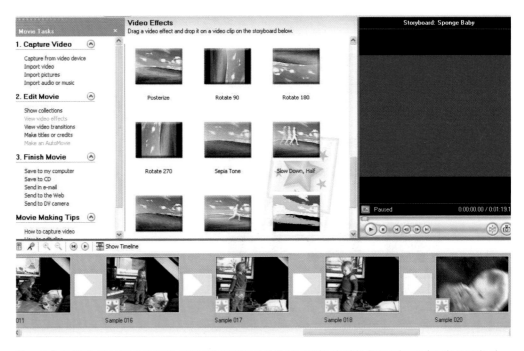

Figure 1.2.120 *By playing both at the same time it is easier to decide the volume levels required for each*

Figure 1.2.121 *The Audio Levels control*

Adding narration

Narration cannot be added at the same point as music. If narration is required, it needs to be added to a part of the film which does not have another soundtrack. Of course, you can edit the soundtrack to contain the narration, as you did earlier, then add this to the video.

Click on the **Narrate Timeline** tool.

Figure 1.2.122 The Narrate Timeline tool is above the Storyboard view

Position the line at the point where the narration is to begin (Figure 1.2.123). It may be necessary to trim the soundtrack that you added previously. Click on **Start Narration**. Talk until you have the narration required then click on **Stop Narration** (Figure 1.2.124).

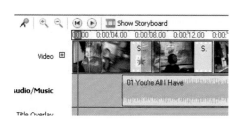

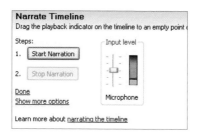

Figure 1.2.123 Position the cursor at the start point

Figure 1.2.124 The sound level with fluctuate as audio is added

A dialog box asking you to save the narration will appear. Give it a sensible name and click on **Save**, after which the narration will be added to the timeline.

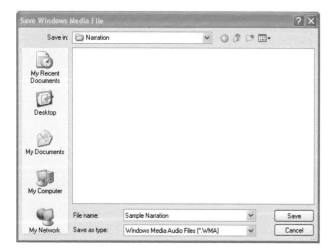

Figure 1.2.125 Save the newly created narration

It is a good idea to play the movie and adjust the volume so that the narration can be heard clearly.

Adding titles and credits

For any film, the title needs to be shown at the start and the credits for those who were involved in production at the end.

To add a title at the start of the film select **Make titles or credits** (Figure 1.2.126). Choose **Add title at the beginning of the movie** (Figure 1.2.127).

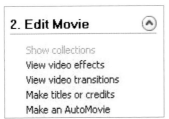

Figure 1.2.126 Use this menu to access the credit options

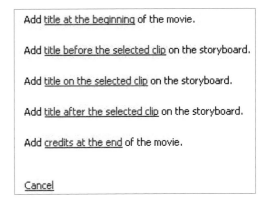

Figure 1.2.127 Select the first option

Add the title of the film in the blank space provided. Experiment with the title animation, text font, and colour until it is as desired. The title can be previewed on the viewing panel on the right and will appear on the timeline.

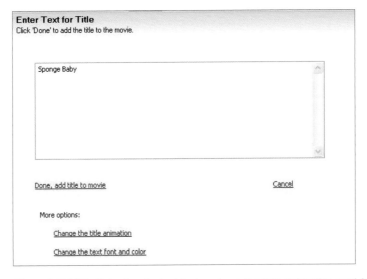

Figure 1.2.128 Enter the desired text and use the text animation and font options to enhance the text

When you're finished, click on **Done** to add the title to the movie.

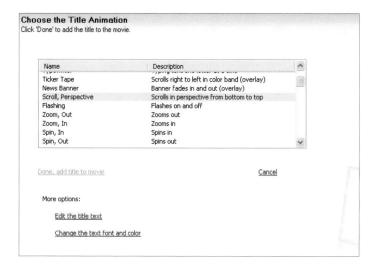

Figure 1.2.129 *Play the credit or title to see if it performs the task required*

Follow the same process to add titles to other parts of the film by choosing different options from the menu below.

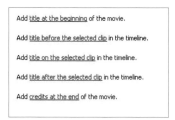

Figure 1.2.130 *Experiment with alternative options from the menu*

Credits can be produced, and these are automatically added to the end of the film.

Figure 1.2.131 *The end and start of the film show the credits added to the film*

Saving the file as a movie

Click on **Save to my computer**.

Figure 1.2.132 The save menu

Enter a file name and select the location where the file is to be stored.

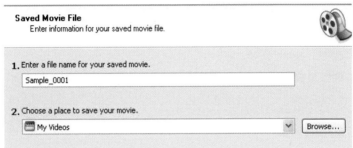

Figure 1.2.133 Enter the name for the finished film

Then select **Next** twice. The following screen shows the movie being converted for viewing.

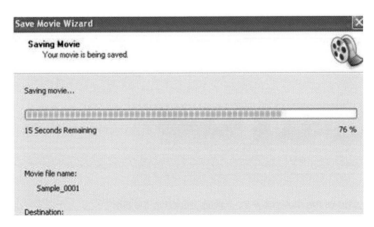

Figure 1.2.134 The larger the file the longer the save process will take

When it is finished, completely close Movie Maker, navigate to the file and double click on it to see how your movie looks.

If you now wanted to save it to a portable medium, the film can be burnt onto a DVD or CD using alternative software like Nero StartSmart or saved onto a pen drive.

1.2.11 Image manipulation software

Images are a graphical representation of data. When an image is used for a purpose other than the one for which it was originally intended, it may not be in a form that the audience will understand or appreciate. In such situations it may be necessary to enhance the image. This section deals with the use of images in Adobe Photoshop CS2, although the following instructions can be used with Fireworks too to perform similar actions.

Before starting it is recommended that access to several images is available.

Cropping an image

A captured image may have sections which are not required in the altered version. The cropping tool should be used to remove them, leaving only the sections that are required.

First open an image by going to **File** > **Open**, navigating to and selecting the required image, and clicking **Open**.

Figure 1.2.135 Selecting the required image

The screen has a main toolbar on the left and **Color**, **History** and **Layer** options on the right.

After opening the image, it may be necessary to extend the size of the image by dragging the right hand corner of the frame.

Figure 1.2.136 Enlarging the image makes it easier to work on in more detail

To crop the image, select the **Crop** tool from the toolbar on the left hand side.

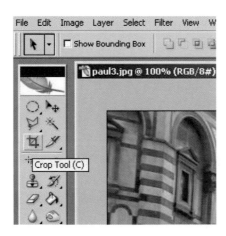

Figure 1.2.137 Selecting the crop tool

Draw over the area that is to be kept. This can be worked on until the desired area fills the light part of the drawn box.

When the area has been selected, right click on the image and select **Crop**, or double click, and the image will be cropped to the selection.

Figure 1.2.138 Ensure the area you want to crop has been left out of the selection

Figure 1.2.139 The image after cropping

The Zoom tool

To work on smaller sections of the image, the **Zoom** tool should be deployed. To zoom in, click on the magnifying glass (Figure 1.2.140), then click on the part of the image you want to zoom in on (Figure 1.2.141).

Figure 1.2.140 Select the magnifying glass tool

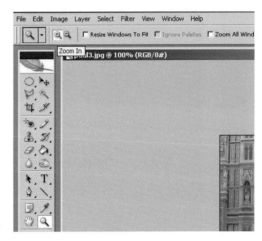

Figure 1.2.141 Use the plus or minus icons to zoom in or out

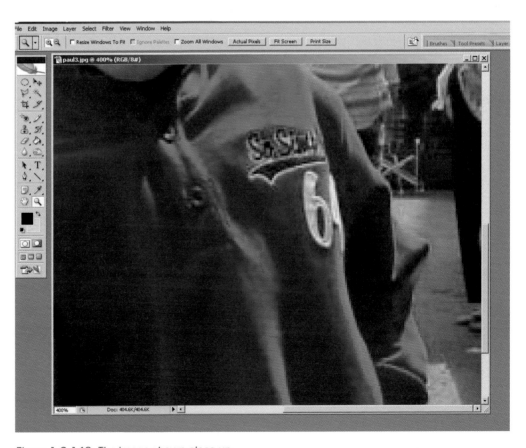

Figure 1.2.142 The image shown close up

Selecting an area to manipulate

To change a specific area, it is necessary to select it by using the followings tools. The **Select** tools enable you to, for example, cut one person's head from one image and place it on another. Then, using the **Blur** and **Color** tools it can be blended in to look like it belongs where it has been placed. By using the same tools, eye colour can be changed, teeth made whiter and, given enough time, hair removed or added (Figure 1.2.143). To view further selection tool options, hold down, then right click the icon (Figures 1.2.144 and 1.2.145).

Figure 1.2.143
Locate the select tool

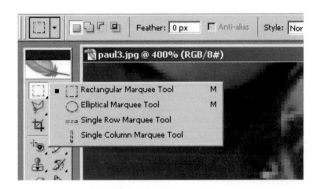

Figure 1.2.144 Keep the right mouse key depressed to view the select options

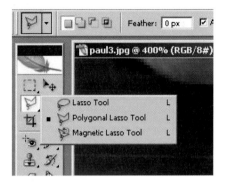

Figure 1.2.145 To draw around areas use this option

It is worth experimenting with these tools to see how they work. For this example, the numbers on the red jumper will be selected and blended into the rest of the red top.

Using the **Polygonal Lasso Tool** click and draw around the area required. To join the polygon at the end of the outline, double click.

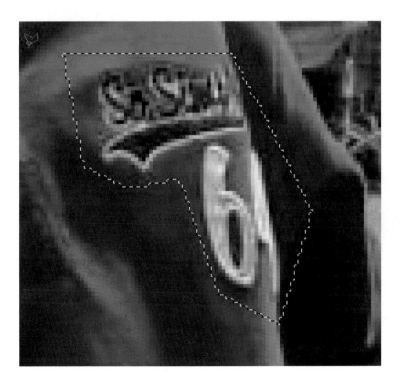

Figure 1.2.146 Take care to draw around everything you want to edit

To remove the selected area, click **Delete** and it will disappear.

Figure 1.2.147 *The selected area has been removed*

The blank area will need to be filled in using a variety of blend, smudge and colour selecting tools. This requires a lot of experimentation because the red top has more than one simple colour and shade.

Using colour to fill the gap

The first step is to select the colour with which to fill the space. The best way to do this is to use the Eyedropper to select a colour already on the top.

Click on the **Eyedropper Tool** (Figure 1.2.148). Then click on the colour which would best fill the gap. This will be displayed in the **Set foreground color** options square (Figure 1.2.149). For this example, the red garment was clicked on.

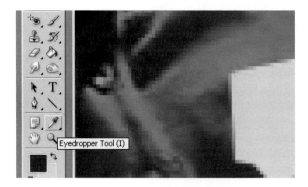

Figure 1.2.148 *Select the Eyedropper tool*

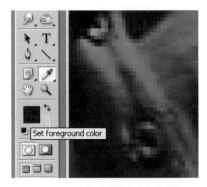

Figure 1.2.149 *Click on the image to gather the best colour option*

The next tool to use is the **Brush** or **Pencil Tool**.

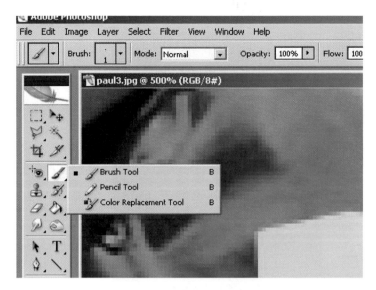

Figure 1.2.150 Remember to keep the right mouse button depressed to expose the options

When selected, the area that can be covered in one click can be increased or decreased by using the following options.

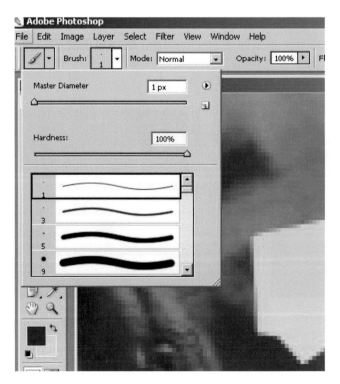

Figure 1.2.151 Varying sizes will fill or colour bigger areas depending on what has been selected

The area to cover is quite big in this case so the point 5 option has been chosen. The next step is to use the mouse to colour the blank area. It will not be perfect at this stage.

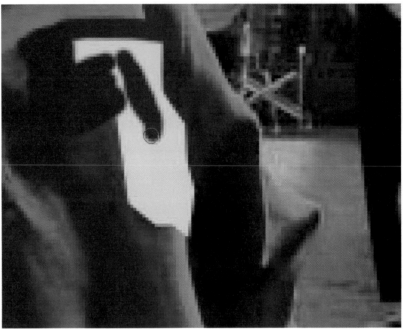

Figure 1.2.152 Use the mouse to colour the blank area

A quicker option for colouring in the blank area would be to select the **Paint Bucket Tool** (Figure 1.2.153) and then click just once in the blank area. When the gap has been coloured, it will need blending in. To do this, the tools shown in Figure 1.2.154 can be used.

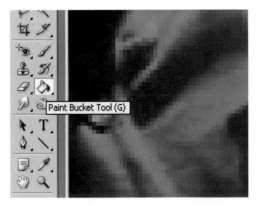

Figure 1.2.153 Select the Paint Bucket tool

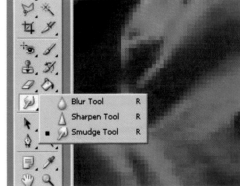

Figure 1.2.154 Selecting the tools to blend colour together

By selecting the **Blur** or **Smudge Tool**, the mouse can be rubbed over the coloured area to help blend it in. Please note this is an introduction to the tools and the results will not be perfect at this stage. By zooming in and selecting smaller areas and different shades, a more polished, finished look can be achieved.

Figure 1.2.155 Time, care and effort are required to get a really good finish

To check your progress, use the **Zoom** tool to zoom out.

Figure 1.2.156 Always check the overall image to see how it looks

Using the Filter options

To add a new dimension to an image, select the **Filter** menu and experiment with the options there. The whole image can be worked on in one go or you can choose to select an area.

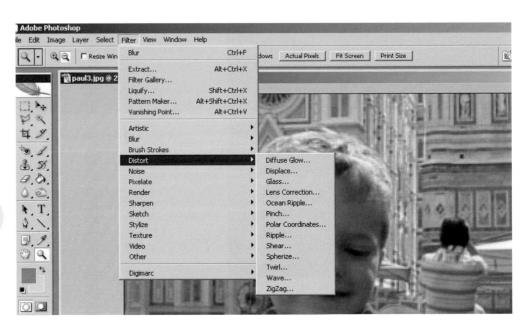

Figure 1.2.157 *The Filter menu is extensive but intuitive to use*

The area behind the boy has been selected using the **Polygonal Lasso Tool**.

Figure 1.2.158 *Note the dotted lines used to show what has been selected*

For the next step, go to **Filter** > **Artistic** > **Dry Brush**.

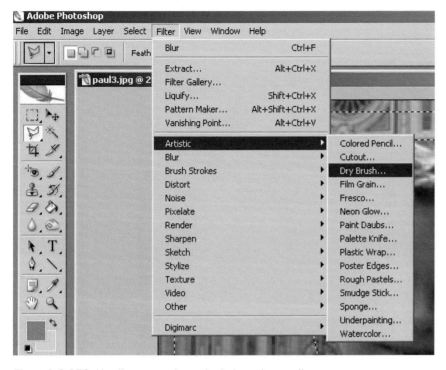

Figure 1.2.159 *Use the mouse to navigate to various options*

The following options appear, giving the opportunity to look at alternatives. For this image, the **Fresco** look was ultimately selected.

Figure 1.2.160 *Again, alternatives can be experimented with using the mouse*

When you are satisfied with the image, click **OK** and view the image. To improve it further, zoom in and use the **Blur** and **Smudge** tools.

Figure 1.2.161 *Remember to use the blending tools to smarten up the edges*

Adding text

In some cases, your image may require a caption or other text.

Click on the **Type Tool** icon and select the most appropriate option.

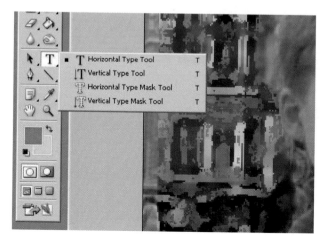

Figure 1.2.162 *Selecting the Type tool*

Position the cursor where you want the text to appear. Type the caption then highlight it, and use the formatting tools to change the font style, size and other attributes.

Figure 1.2.163 *The formatting tools can be altered to give alternative text display*

The text can be moved to another part of the image using the **Move Tool**.

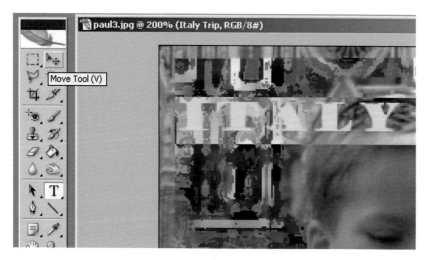

Figure 1.2.164 *By repositioning and sizing the text the impact of the image can be changed*

Click on the **Move Tool**, then click on the text and place it where you want it.

Figure 1.2.165 In this case the text is placed at the bottom of the screen so as not to obscure the image

To complete the image, the size can be adjusted by selecting **Image** > **Image Size** and adding in the required measurements. The image may have to fit a picture frame, a frame on a website or space in a newsletter, and knowing the details beforehand will save time later.

Figure 1.2.166 The Image Size dialog box

The final image can be saved as a JPEG using **File** > **Save As**. Select the JPEG format from the **Format** drop-down list and give the image a sensible file name.

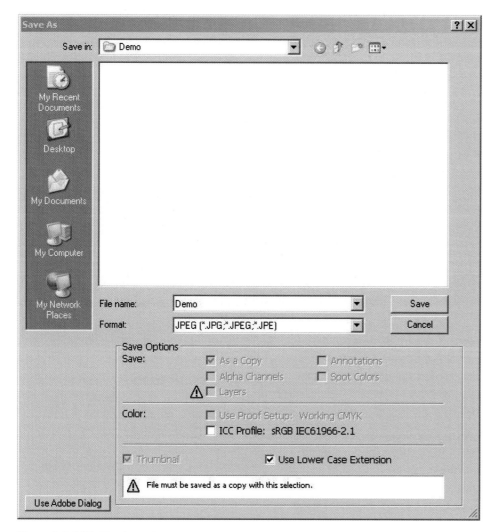

Figure 1.2.167 The Save As dialog box

By experimenting with the tools, it is possible to create buttons and banners with text or a front cover for a magazine. It is worth spending some time with this software and experimenting with the tools. It can be frustrating at times, but with practice and effort it is possible to make real improvements and stunning images.

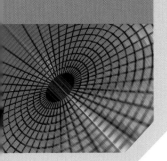

1.3 Presenting information and disseminating it

1.3.1 Text

Textual information is the written form. It can be presented in printed hard copy as a document, report, newsletter or a book, or presented electronically as a document screen, on a website, as an email, or as a file on a removable or non-removable storage medium.

There are many options available to you that allow you to control the presentation of a text file – the font, size and colour of the text being the simplest ones – but text can also be presented in tabular format and it can be emphasised through emboldening a title, underlining an important phrase or italicising a term.

Combinations of data are discussed in a later section, but for the moment it is important to accept the importance of textual data in the choice of presentation method and the method of dissemination.

As with all presentations of data, the audience and purpose of the output must be taken into account – a report for a board of directors may use a formal report structure, with an executive summary, contents pages, sectionalised main body and an index. Headers and footers will be used and it may use a company template. Memos, faxes, agendas and minutes may also have their own templates. Most word-processing packages offer a range of standard templates for use, or a business may design their own. The language in these documents may also be formal; many companies have rules about style, preferring, for instance, for a report to always be written in the third person.

A newsletter for company employees may have a less formal look, with snippets of news positioned in a publishing template to look more like a newspaper or magazine, possibly using columns. Language in such a document may be less formal and more colloquial.

A printed document can be handed to another person, sent through the internal mail or posted to particular recipients. Other printed items might be leaflets, for example flyers for local businesses, which are dropped through letter boxes or left in public places for people to pick up. Other ways of disseminating printed materials are in a shop where books, papers and magazines are for sale.

Within businesses, printed documents may be preferred over electronic documents in such instances where the document is legally binding and needs a signature, e.g. contracts; where the document is to be used by a group of people at the same time, e.g. within a meeting; or where the contents of the document are confidential and potential widespread electronic dissemination is not desired.

Emails are another example of textual writing. The text is generally keyed straight into the email package, a recipient's address is added, and the email is sent. Better packages have the facility to spell-check the text, but it is often not used, indicating that the medium is not generally considered to be a formal means of communication. Text files can be sent as attachments to emails – the recipient is at liberty to read the electronic document on-screen or to print it out for their own records.

For regular computer users, reading text on-screen is an everyday task. This can be as a result of opening a file which contains text, reading an email, looking at the results of a search engine query, opening up a website, and so on. There are still many mainly text sites that hold information that will help us in our job or quest for more information on a topic.

As pure text files tend to be small, an easy physical method of passing them from person to person – or originating machine to receiving machine – could be on a floppy disk. However, given that these are little used nowadays, many

Figure 1.3.1

text files could be transferred on either a USB pen drive or a CD-ROM or CD-RW. If it was important not to erase the file after transferring it to a target machine, a CD-ROM would need to be used.

Presentation software is often used to produce text-only shows to be projected onto a screen, using a data projector, or shown on an interactive whiteboard. This method of information dissemination can be used in all situations, from showing the presentation to one or more people huddled around a PC, to a class full of attentive students, to a conference hall filled with a few hundred delegates.

1.3.2 Numbers

Numeric data needs to be presented in a format that is meaningful to the reader of the data, and so is normally presented in some sort of tabular format or graphically, as a chart or graph.

Accounting or spreadsheet software is normally used to manipulate numerical data. The features and functions of these packages are designed to make 'number-crunching' as easy as possible for the user. Of course, numerical data can be used in other software, such as word-processing packages (some of which have the ability to do simple calculations based on tabulated numerical data) and database management software, which usually has the ability to perform calculations in much the same way as spreadsheet functions, as part of the query process or even on reports and forms.

If displaying numeric data in a tabular format then the columns, and perhaps the rows, need to have labels – otherwise, the data is meaningless. The example league tables in Figure 1.3.2 are the result of a spreadsheet application that allows scores to be entered and then processed to calculate the final results. The data has been sorted on points gained to provide the full picture.

U16A Table

Team	P	W	D	L	F	A	Points
Fletcher Moss	8	6	1	1	32	15	13
Flixton	8	4	1	3	32	20	9
Stretford Victoria	5	4	0	1	27	16	8
De La Salle	8	3	2	3	20	24	8
Sale United 'A'	6	1	1	4	9	21	3
Manchester Eagles	7	0	1	6	18	42	1

U16B Table

Team	P	W	D	L	F	A	Points
Oswald Road	9	5	2	2	32	20	12
Broadheath Central	8	4	2	2	26	14	10
Sale United 'B'	9	3	3	3	22	23	9
Gorse Hill Lads	10	2	5	3	20	26	9
Urmston Town	6	1	4	1	13	11	6
Wilmslow Sports	8	2	0	6	18	37	4

Figure 1.3.2 Tabular display

Displaying data in graphical format is quite easy in a spreadsheet package that has the facilities to create charts and graphs. There is usually a wide range of chart and graph styles to choose from. The example balance sheet in Figure 1.3.3 shows just a few of the graph styles that are available:

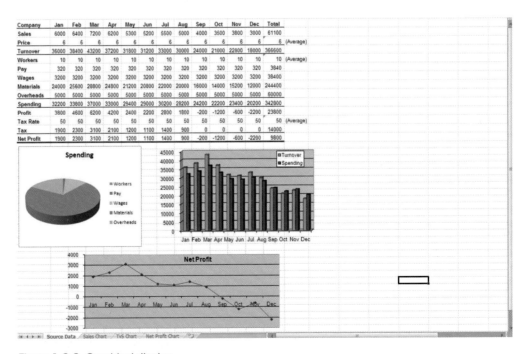

Figure 1.3.3 Graphical display

The ways of presenting numerical data to an audience are similar to those for textual data. It is almost impossible to display numerical data without using text, as numbers on their own, and unexplained, would be mostly meaningless to the viewer. Thus, numeric data can be found in hard copy as printed forms within reports, documents, newsletters, and so on. It can also be displayed on websites or as part of a presentation.

Spreadsheet files, even quite complex multi-sheet applications, rarely take up more than a megabyte of space and so can be disseminated in all of the usual ways without causing any problems.

1.3.3 Sounds

When a sound file is finally in the state desired by its producer, it can be disseminated in a number of ways.

There are many examples of software available for preparing sounds for transfer to a media which will play it. Sounds can be burnt onto CD or DVDs and played repeatedly. They can be layered over video footage to create tension or any other feeling the director wants to evoke. Sounds can be attached as files to web pages for people to play or download.

Sounds are also a large part of the presentation of some web pages. The act of using hyperlinks from one page to another may trigger a sound file to introduce the new page. Sound files on web pages may also provide a commentary to the user about the latest product.

Sounds can be downloaded onto computer systems and, by attaching speakers, can be played to an audience of a few or thousands. This will largely depend on the quality of the speakers used, which make up the most vital aspect of presenting sound. Without speakers, audio files cannot be heard, therefore consideration of the audience size and location needs to be given. A small, humble desktop set of speakers will not generate enough amplification to cover a large conference room, while spending thousands on surround sound speakers for a small classroom may be frivolous and expensive.

The alternative to listening to sound in public is the private enjoyment to be gained from listening to tracks, shows and news. Modern music players accept digital versions of sounds and play them back with a crisp, clear quality. Joggers wear such devices on their arm or clipped to their running vest, taking for granted the fact that the track won't jump, be chewed up or fall out of inferior casing.

MP3 players accept play lists from computer systems and give the user the flexibility to jump from track to track, play the music in a random order, or as the artist intended. The music is played through headphones, which come in a vast array of shapes and sizes. Some fit over and into the ears while others cover half the wearer's head. Headphones can be wireless, giving the wearer the freedom to move around, but this technology is limited by the range of the source of the signal.

Evidence of prepared sounds can be found in all sorts of situations:

- Underground stations play looped sounds which warn commuters to 'Mind the gap' or that 'There are delays on the Northern line'. Sensors trip communication systems into broadcasting 'The next stop will be . . .' messages.

- Above ground, sound files are now played in parking spaces reserved for certain categories of driver. For instance, child spaces are reserved for those shopping with young children in supermarkets' or shoppers' car parks. A speaker built into a robust steel pole plays a message asking drivers if the space they have taken is really for them.

- Air stewardesses play sound files and perform a routine prior to the aircraft joining the skies. The advantage in this instance is that by using the same recording over and over again, the likelihood of missing out key survival details is reduced to nothing.

Commercially, there is a massive market consisting of people and businesses who want to listen to news from radio shows uploaded onto radio station websites. The ability to download the latest news and have it read to you means no more struggling to read the newspaper on the Tube. The ability to download the most popular music at any given time is appealing and it is cheaper to buy a single now then it was in the 1980s! Some albums may only have 3 tracks in which the buyer is interested – previously the fan would have had to buy the whole album. Digital technology means that we can all be a bit more fussy and select and pay for those tunes, and only those tunes, that we want to hear.

The sounds available in digital or any other format would have been produced for a reason. It may have been a simple message of good tidings sent to a relative as an email attachment. It may be a transcript of an essay which is to be assessed by a blind lecturer. Teenagers are becoming

more adept at using software to produce dance tracks in their bedrooms. They are able to collect samples, weave them together, convert them into sound files like MP3s and download them onto their own or friends' MP3 players. The same tune can be uploaded to specific websites for others to listen to and pass judgement.

Sounds can be given away free or bought for a fee. The option to charge or not to charge is often with the producer. A company that invests millions of pounds in a recording artist are only going to recoup their investment by charging for what the artist has produced. Sound artists who painstakingly collect sounds from nature, airports or any other public place are performing a service which may help generate a fee from those who could benefit from having access to those sounds.

1.3.4 Still images

When an image has been captured, manipulated and prepared, it is ready for public or private viewing. Images appear in all sorts of places and are often used to reduce the number of words needed to convey a message. A poorly edited or out of focus image can reduce its intended impact and value.

Figure 1.3.4 BBC iPlayer

Images of celebrities merely walking into a shop are paid for by popular culture magazines while other images are used to sell products. In every case the image needs to be appropriate for its intended use. Even if the intended subject of the picture has been captured, the image may have been taken from too far away, which will affect its clarity and usefulness. The need to be able to identify what the picture is supposed to be showing is crucial.

Advertisers use images to help promote and sell products. The final image has to be clear and make the point that the advertisers are hoping to make. Images are often published in a variety of sizes and formats, from tiny, passport photo-sized pictures on a driving licence to massive billboards along motorways, which are supposed to attract the eye of potential customers who may be travelling by bus, taxi or in their own car.

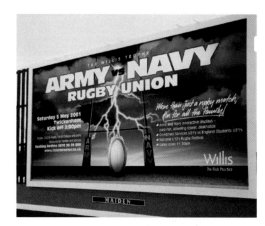

Figure 1.3.5 Billboard advert (from http://www.podigroup.co.uk/50/billboard-advertising.aspx)

Images are used by journalists to help explain a news story. In this instance, the commonly referred to paparazzi are notorious for collecting pictures in the hope of later selling them on to broadcasting news outlets. Mobile phones allow passers-by to photograph or film crimes taking place. Such images become very valuable to news stations who want to be the first to show any firsthand evidence which can add credibility to a story. Once they have the images, the news channels can edit and build them into news reports.

The use of the Internet has exploded in the last decade. Static, text-based pages have been replaced by vibrant, image-dominated sites. Images can be clicked on to open up further pages to give more information. Rather than having to look through masses of text, Internet users have been inadvertently acclimatised to looking for an image which makes the most sense in relation to what they are looking for. Retailers who sell a whole fashion range will include images of as many products as they can. Often an image of a shoe, dress, hat, bag or accessory will be shown on the homepage. A click on the hat will open up the area of the site which deals with hats only. Further thumbnail images may be shown which can also be clicked for further details.

The use of images has greatly improved the way in which we interface with computers. Retailers use pictures of their products to add navigation while the likes of Microsoft and Apple use images of folders, a big blue E, a picture of a printer and other recognisable icons to aid the use of software. If the image is not instantly recognisable, it may not attract further attention or could lead to confusion.

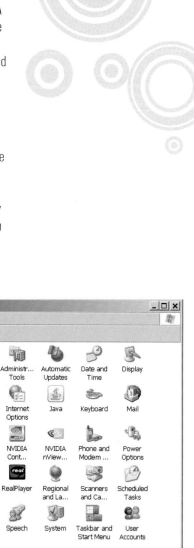

Figure 1.3.6 Control Panel

Images can be used as evidence. Some organisations try to tell the public one version of a story because it may reduce the impact that the truth could have. However images often prove that what is being said is not actually what happened. In criminal cases, photographic evidence can be produced from still CCTV footage. When faced with a series of good quality images which show somebody approach a car, smash the window and steal a bag, clearly showing the suspect's face, the charges become somewhat hard to deny. It may be possible to claim the images are fakes; therefore, the reliability of the source will need to be verified before it can be submitted as evidence. There are experts who make a living from being able to prove whether an image is genuine or has been altered using image manipulation software.

Traditionally, photo albums were normally used to organise pictures taken at family occasions like holidays, weddings or parties. Now it is not uncommon for these to be cropped, have the contrast changed and size increased on a home PC, and then stored in a digital photo album. Such albums allow photographs to be labelled and placed into categories for searching at a later date.

By purchasing photographic paper, selected images can be printed at home and can be shared amongst the family at a fraction of the cost of reproducing an entire album. Alternatively, a CD-ROM containing the whole album can be sent to faraway family members for their own use.

Other places that images can be seen surround the public everyday. Book, DVD and CD covers are carefully designed to catch the potential customer's attention. Dull-coloured book covers do not encourage readers to pick them up. The cover usually gives a clue about what or who the book is about. Science fiction, fantasy, sport and cookery all follow a simple formula which the readers are generally expecting to see on each front cover. Photographs of recording artists might be featured on the front of their CD offerings, often taken at great expense and using the best equipment.

In order for the finished image to carry full impact, the printing phase has to be carefully considered. Wedding photographers do not supply the memories of the happy day on basic A4 plain paper. This reduces the visual shine of the image. Likewise, fashion magazines use the best quality paper which shows off their product range to the best effect. They are not called glossies by accident. Billboard posters have to endure all kinds of weather and remain fixed in place. Photographic or normal printer paper would be no good for this.

1.3.5 Moving images

There has already been a brief discussion relating to the capture of moving images, which excluded Shrek and other animated films due to the fact that they are created on computer systems and screens and it is not possible to physically capture them in real life. However, at this stage the purpose is to explore the outputs which incorporate moving images and animated films are included.

After moving images are collected and edited together, they are ready for presentation to whichever audience the creator decides. The duration of the film will vary from one to another and will convey different information. Films are displayed and produced for a specified purpose which means that the needs of the audience require careful consideration.

A film full of technology jargon delivered by a man in a brown jumper for one hour in front of a blackboard is not going to appeal to everyone. Most shows for teenagers barely hold the same screen shot for longer than 3 seconds. Flashing and changing images appear to be designed to suit younger audiences. Young children are presented with colourful images, friendly faces and shows which last around 15 minutes – any longer than this and they may lose interest.

Moving images can be in the form of animations. Shrek animations, for example, have been painstakingly produced by graphic artists over many months or years. It is common practice today for many people to be working on one animation motion picture as this reduces the time it takes to complete the movie.

There are many different outlets for moving images and these will vary depending on the purpose. Information the BBC wants us all to be aware of, like how to purchase a TV licence, is frequently broadcast.

Commercial organisations take advantage of moving images commonly played on DVD. Short training videos can be produced by an independent organisations which might detail the change in employment laws for UK residents. This film can be purchased by an interested company and played to all their staff over a number of days and months to bring them up to speed with the change in legislation.

Educational institutions take advantage of this media as well, and it would be difficult to find a teacher or lecturer who has not used motion pictures to reinforce a message or add a different dimension to what they are trying to explain. Many documentaries and films can be captured by DVD recorders, so they can be saved and used whenever required. They can also be transferred onto laptops and shown in small groups or projected to a larger audience.

With the help of some bright young minds, music videos can now be accessed online on popular sites and viewed at request. Apple have created an MP3 player with a small screen which can

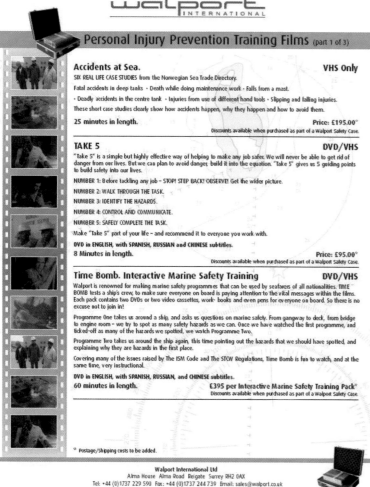

Figure 1.3.7 Training video (from http://www.walport.co.uk/public/catalogue_brochures.php)

accept music and videos downloaded from its online store for a nominal fee which can be viewed time and time again. Technology that fits in trouser pockets, like the iPhone and many other mobile phones, also have small screens which are big enough to allow the viewer to see moving images clearly.

Moving images can be projected on or seen through huge screens. A good example of this can be seen at sporting venues that replay events soon after something has happened. Some officials have found this very useful as it often help them to see more clearly who has won a race. At the other end of the spectrum is the poor football referee who repeatedly has his blunders played back to the entire crowd of thousands; there is nowhere to hide in the instant playback world! Images can be zoomed into, played back and paused and a decision made.

Figure 1.3.8 Replay

There are many websites on the Internet which include videos that provided further information, instructions or opinions. This technology has been utilised by TV stations that allow viewers to log in and watch programmes they may have missed. A good example of where this is useful is when travellers abroad want to keep up-to-date with current affairs. They can access the Newsnight website and watch the most recent show or choose from a selection.

On websites such as Youtube.com, anyone can upload motion images including music, short films, and home videos of people tripping over hedges. Aspiring Hollywood directors use the site to showcase their personal endeavours and get their work seen by millions. Exercise routines are only a keyword search away, which means that finding a local expert for fitness advice, at cost, may not be required. News footage from years ago can be displayed and played back, and referenced as research by students.

Moving images allow the viewer to see what a certain situation was actually like. The horrific scenes of the twin towers being brought tumbling down can take pages of text to describe, but within a few seconds the full horror can be witnessed from many different camera angles and speeds.

Documentaries lasting one hour are often the result of refining many hours of footage. A prudent viewer will appreciate this and will realise that the message could be drastically altered had an alternative director been used. The producers of adverts, short films, movies, documentaries or any type of show designed for public viewing have edited clips to be seen in a certain way. If a politician is filmed punching the local electorate, this is more likely to be broadcast by the news station than if he had gone about normal electioneering. The provocation for the punch may be omitted by some channels and commented on by others. The punches thrown by the politician may be shown and the retaliation by the public omitted. The message in each situation can be altered just enough to make the viewer think or feel differently about what they have seen.

When set down as a video file on a computer system or burnt onto a VCD or DVD the film can be viewed, copied and transferred time after time.

When home users pick up the digital video camera and start filming the family, the intended audience is already known and the purpose is usually to capture moments for posterity. The option to burn a whole library of DVDs as a generation of children grow up is now in the hands of personal computer users. They are only limited by their own ability to make the captured footage into something more dramatic with some exciting voice-overs and music.

Live streams of moving images are shown on a daily basis on the web and TV. News reporters often report direct from battle zones and people use web cameras at home to add to their VOIP software so that they can see who they are talking to over the Internet.

1.3.6 Combining types for output

Combining different types of data for presentation is witnessed on a regular basis. Text, sound, animation and video footage are often presented together to convey a range of messages and information. The obvious example is a TV advert which features real world footage combined with animation, a voice-over and some form of text tying it all together to form one product.

It is not always necessary to use every form of data to get a message over. Sometimes a simple pie chart with text in the title gives the viewers all the information they need. The quality of the information conveyed will be diminished if it is not produced with the particular audience in mind. Producing a 300 page text-only document about the year's trading figures, to give to a busy managing director, is likely to go unread. The information in this case needs to be given in illustrations under clear headings which can be located from an index or contents page.

A presentation can incorporate dynamic data files, which are real-time links to data in other packages, for example spreadsheets. The data in the spreadsheet package can be updated during the presentation and the effects can be seen immediately within the presentation. Hyperlinks to web pages can also be incorporated so the web page can be shown to demonstrate a relevant point without going in and out of the presentation software. Images and text are regularly combined on one slide. These are all examples of combining data for output.

Images are often combined with a short caption, which quickly explains what it is about or where

Figure 1.3.9 Combining data – hyperlink

Figure 1.3.10 Combining data – web link

it came from. Audio and visual data are often combined as a way to show and tell information. Text and audio are combined in the form of audio books. CDs or tapes are sold along with books which are used to help people learn to read or to learn a language. They can be paused, rewound and practised time after time.

Simple or complex animation can add appeal to interactive software for adults or children. A talking dragon acting as a guide through a series of history-based lessons may be more interesting to young children than listening to their teacher. Animation is also used with sound and audio to display how a particular planet or period of time may have looked millions of years ago. It is not physically possible to show real footage of some places and this is where the use of animation can be useful.

There are many examples of learning resources which combine different forms of data. Text can give initial information, images can act as navigations aids, sound effects announce when a new level is reached and moving images (animated or real) can show demonstrations and interact with the user. Processing test scores and reward certificates helps to complete the package.

The Internet has given the world's media, advertisers and everyone else the forum to demonstrate multiple examples of combined data. As is the case for all types of data, the purpose for forming an output needs to be decided upon first. When this is agreed, the method of getting the information across can be investigated.

Advertisers like to hit all the senses when pushing a new product at consumers. The use of music is often prevalent. Text laid over moving images and choice words delivered at predefined frames add to the impact of a good advert. Speeding up or slowing down motion can vastly improve the way the finished advert is perceived, and even the positioning of text on the screen is carefully tested before release.

When data assets are combined, a whole range of software can be exploited to improve the quality of the final product. Size, style, shape and colour of text as well as the actual text used need to be figured out. Sound in the form of a voice-over or music has to be cut, edited and positioned with precision to the smallest allowable part of a second. Regional accent, tone, pitch, speed and volume are tried and matched to the text. Sometimes the audio will be different to the text which means several outputs are being given out simultaneously. Any moving images which rely on text appearing at different frames needs to be tested thoroughly so as to avoid key parts of the screen output being obscured by oversized text. The speed and timing of music or narration and on screen images are layered together, played back, repositioned and edited until all the assets are in the right place and give the desired message.

The ability to combine information to deliver a message can be in the simple form of a sound-activated birthday card, or a full scale motion picture. The limitations are often attributed to the available software, the user's imagination and time. Failing to properly establish the best method for providing particular information and the audience's needs could seriously undermine the intended message by either drowning it in special effects or underplaying it with a dull delivery.

Section 2
Contexts

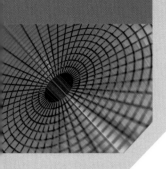

2.1 Introduction

There are many different types of problems that can be solved using digital means and in this section we examine a number of diverse scenarios and suggest alternative ways of solving them. If there is a 'best' solution then it is highlighted, but in many instances it is down to the preference of the developer or the availability of the hardware and software tools.

Examples of the type of problems that can be solved through digital means are:

- record keeping

- analysing results

- presenting information to different audiences (local or distant)

- presenting different types of information (images, text, video)

- communicating with different audiences (local or distant)

- communicating in different ways (sound only, sound and image, text only, pre-recorded sound, pre-recorded sound and image, etc.)

- Manipulating sounds, images, etc.

Just taking these examples, it is easy to draw up a possible list of software that might solve the problem type, for example:

Problem	Choice	Solution	Some possible software
Record keeping	1	Database	MS Access Open Office – Base
	2	Database function of spreadsheet	MS Excel OpenOffice – Calc
Presenting information to local audiences	1	Electronic presentation	MS PowerPoint OpenOffice – Impress Mediator
	2	Text-based	MS Word OpenOffice – Writer Publisher
	3	Interactive whiteboards	Smart

Problem	Choice	Solution	Some possible software
Presenting information to distant audiences	1	Website	Dreamweaver
			Mediator
			Flash
			FrontPage
			Netscape Composer
			Adobe GoLive
			Any HTML or XML editor
Recording and presenting speech	1	Podcast	Podium
			Podcast Wizard
Recording and presenting sound	1	Sound file (MP3, WMF, etc)	Audacity (Open source)
			Sound Forge Audio Studio 9
			Sound Studio (MAC OS X)
			Windows sound recorder
Recording and presenting video	1	Video	Windows Movie Maker
			Sony Vegas Movie Studio 8
			Adobe Premiere Elements 4
Presenting images	1	Photo album	Picasa
			HDMS-S1D Digital Photo Album
			Ulead Photo Explorer 8
			Photo Story 3 – free from Microsoft
	2	Slide show	PowerPoint
			OpenOffice – Impress
			Mediator
			Photo Story 3 – free from Microsoft
	3	Web pages	Fireworks
			Digital Image
			Expression Web
Manipulating images	1		Adobe Photoshop
			GIMP (Open source)
			Graphic Design Studio
			CorelDRAW
			Fireworks

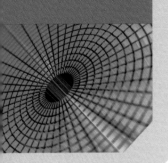

2.2 Rolling multimedia presentation for a school open day

Current situation

Morton Weaver is a small secondary school that has excellent sporting facilities including several well-groomed cricket, rugby and football pitches. They usually have 300 pupils on roll, and are located next to a river which allows them to train rowers. Some have gone on to represent Britain at the Olympics. The staff at Morton Weaver have recently been encouraged to undertake more professional development to encourage them to stay abreast of the current trends in promoting good teaching and learning. As a result, the standard of lessons delivered was praised during a recent inspection, and academic results have also improved. The school has a very good ICT network with a computer for every teacher in each classroom, three rooms with twenty machines each and seven small satellite areas with three or four machines in each, all running the same software.

The school has been promised a generous donation provided it can sustain its numbers and increases its roll by an extra twenty pupils per year. The management at Morton Weaver believes that this can be achieved by promoting the school within the local area by inviting prospective parents to come and visit and see the facilities on offer. The school is confident that they have the personnel to run frequent open days and are keen to use technology as well. There has been a suggestion that software could be used to showcase the school electronically, by putting together a presentation which can be viewed by visiting parents while they wait to talk to a member of staff. A working party has asked that the presentation include details relating to staff training, sports facilities and opportunities, and the improving academic record. It must also be easy to update with new images or current news relating to the school's activities.

In summary – the requirements are:

1 to produce a presentation providing information about the school to local prospective parents

2 to be able to edit and update information after regular reviews

3 to be able to leave the presentation unattended while parents and staff meet

4 to capture the attention of visitors

5 to provide details about the school's sporting achievements and opportunities

6 to provide information relating to the improved teaching and learning

7 to provide information showing the improved academic results

8 to include relevant images to complement any text.

Things to ponder

- Which staff or pupils can provide data to put into the system?

- What data should be included?

- Who will ensure the data included is appropriate?

- How often should data be updated?

- Is the software a required part of the school network? If not, what would be the best option?

- How soon does the presentation need to be ready?

- What size monitor would be best to display the presentation?

- Would a projector be required? If so, what type and where will it/they be?

- Is funding for extra equipment required/available?

- In how many and which locations should the presentation be running?

- Are there network points at these locations?

- Will this system need to have security? Who will ensure that data is refreshed at regular intervals?

- Is there an issue with using images of pupils and staff? If so how do we overcome such issues?

- What might be needed as part of a backup strategy?

Possible approaches to implementation

- Creating a design for a standard screen with a consistent look that is clearly themed to represent Morton Weaver's needs.

- The data is to be updated regularly; therefore, some consideration with regard to creating a store to hold used and new data needs to be investigated. This could be in a simple word-processing document or presentational format.

- The main software used is likely to be presentational software which has a slide show facility, like MS PowerPoint, that can be divided into categories of different types of information and set up to run continuously.

- Alternatives are Apple's Keynote or OpenOffice's Impress. Do these run on the school network and does anyone know how to use them?

The recommendation

For this system, the best option on the current school network which supports MS products is going to be Microsoft PowerPoint. It is quite an intuitive program and most pupils have been taught to use it. The Master Slide facility will mean that some consistency can be achieved from slide to slide, but careful consideration as to the content and look of the master slide must be the first priority. Image manipulation can be done through Adobe Photoshop at an advanced level, or the drawing and cropping tools in PowerPoint may be enough. The option to run the presentation on a loop is built into PowerPoint, as is the option to quickly obtain a range of printouts if parents want to take a hardcopy away.

The issue regarding data storage for material used and to be used in the future can be overcome by setting a series of sensibly labeled folders and carefully considered naming conventions for images and files of text. Dates and version numbers should be used. To ensure that data is incorporated successfully, several people can be trained to edit and update the presentation and a small support manual could be produced in a publishing package.

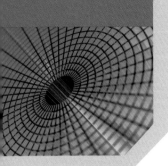

2.3 Producing invoices for a small business

Current situation

A small garage currently has no computer system for producing invoices for its customers, although it does have a PC linked up to the national MOT computerised system, the equipment having been provided for them in 2004 when they got one day's training from the systems developer. They have not touched it since and there is no other software on the PC apart from the operating system.

A diary is currently used to record jobs, MOTs, servicing, repairs and so on, and an invoice is manually written out when the customer comes in to collect their car. Standard prices for particular jobs or cost per hour for particular mechanics are on a list on the office wall, and other prices (for spare parts and so on), are added onto the written invoice at cost price.

The owner of the garage would like to have a database of all customers, a history of past jobs, and the ability to record what was done to a particular vehicle on a particular day, as well as being able to produce an invoice without having to write out all of the details each time.

The other thing they have noticed is that as cars get bought and sold, they sometimes deal with a car that they've worked on before, but on behalf of a different customer.

The owner considers himself and the other mechanics to be novice computer users – they can only do what they have been shown and no more. Any problems and they immediately get professional help.

In summary – the requirements are:

1   to create a customer database

2   to have the ability to add/amend/delete customer details

3   to create a standard task/price list

4   to have the ability to amend prices, add tasks, etc.

5   to record details of a job for a customer (car details, work done, etc.)

6   to see the job history for a car or a customer

7   to produce an invoice for a job.

 Things to ponder

- Cost – is there a budget? Buying software is one option, but it is likely that open source software would be adequate for this fairly straightforward system.

- Is there an Internet connection that could be used to download free software?

- Will it be OK to use the printer currently used for MOT certificates for this system? If a blank A4 MOT form is fed in each time, rather than continuous tractor fed stationery, then

probably 'yes', otherwise they might need to buy a new printer.

- What is the best solution that covers all the requirements and would be easy to use for these novice users?

- Will this system need to have security? Where is the machine situated? Who has access? Who is allowed to use the functionality?

- Will it need to be registered under the Data Protection Act? Need to check what details are to be held – just name and address, or bank or card details for regular customers?

- What might be needed as part of a backup strategy?

- Could the system link into the MOT system? Is this possible or required?

- As there is currently no electronic record of all the customers, they will have to be added as the jobs come in. Maybe the MOT system creates a local data store of customer names and car details that could be transferred over, to save them being typed in twice? This is worth investigating.

Possible approaches to implementation

Firstly a house style for the invoice and a template for the invoice need to be designed, together with a logo, if required. This is the customer-facing document, whereas all other reports are for internal use only.

After this is complere, there are choices to be made for storing the data and for producing the invoice:

- One way would be to produce a database, say in MS Access or OpenOffice Base, which has tables for customer, task-price, and job, plus possibly car details. This certainly would have the facility to store and query all the data, and an invoice could be produced as a report.

- Another way would be to use the database as above, but to link through to a spreadsheet or word-processing package to produce the invoice.

- Using a spreadsheet is a further choice, although it would be harder to manipulate the data in the circumstance that a car is transferred to another customer. But it could be done, and, if implemented cleverly, may be a cheaper option for the garage (being able to buy the small business version of the software, rather than the full-blown professional version that includes the database).

The recommendation

For this system, the neatest way is to use a database option, but the numerical manipulation required for invoice production would be better served by linking the data for a job through to a spreadsheet, using a macro to move the data across, performing the calculations (VAT, discount, etc.) needed to print the invoice in the spreadsheet, and finally transferring the information back to the database to be added to the job history for that car/customer.

Creating the database and basic add/amend/delete functionality is very straightforward and, with the addition of a switchboard and menuing system, would make it easy for novice users. Adding consistent and simple input forms, query forms and output reports could make it the perfect solution for the client.

Any design-from-scratch package, such as Flash, CorelDRAW, or even MS Paint, could be used to produce a logo, or an image could be taken and manipulated in a package such as Adobe Photoshop for this purpose.

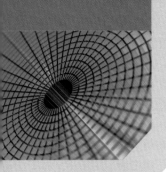

2.4 A systems analyst with RSI using word-processing and specialist software

Current situation

Susan Connor is a systems analyst working for a large pharmaceutical company. For the past two years she has been working with Rational Rose, the data modeling package for entity-relationship design and data modeling, and using word-processing software for producing analysis reports. Both of these packages require a lot of typing and mouse usage. For about 6 months, she has been experiencing wrist and lower arm pains and has been taking painkillers and wearing a wrist support for comfort. The problem has become much worse and she has had to have time off work to see if it improves. The initial diagnosis of Repetitive Strain Injury (RSI) has been confirmed.

However, the work she is involved in is important to the company and they are anxious to get her back working as soon as possible, so need a solution that will enable this. It will have to be a hardware and software solution and they are willing to buy any equipment that she will need. In fact, under the Disability Discrimination Act, they are legally bound to provide a safe work environment with all the facilities that are required for her to continue to do the same job as before.

In summary – the requirements are:

1   an ergonomic work station with features to prevent the RSI from getting worse

2   a software solution so that she can keep on using the software necessary for her job, i.e. as a minimum, MS Office software and Rational Rose

3   any hardware associated with the software

4   a method of ensuring that the Health and Safety aspects are met, to prevent the RSI from recurring

5   a safe and secure working environment.

Things to ponder

- Does sitting position affect RSI?

- Having a natural language interface (voice input) may distract other workers. Will she therefore have to have her own office?

- What can be done to stop her making the RSI worse once she goes back to work?

- How reliable is voice input software?

- What extra equipment is required to use a natural language interface?

- How accurate is this software?

- How can she conduct interviews and gather information which is traditionally done by making handwritten notes?

Possible approaches to implementation

The first aspect of this problem that must be addressed is how to reduce any typing time or mouse usage. This could be done simply by removing the traditional keyboard and mouse and replacing them with ergonomically designed hardware that does the same job. There are many options for ergonomic keyboards, using different shapes for better hand and arm positioning, wrist rests built into the keyboard, larger, less fiddly keys, and so on.

Ergonomic mice range from ones with large, rolling top-side balls with left and right click balls too, to hand-held ones that fit in the palm with click and control buttons at different angles which can be used by thumb and forefinger, to mice that resemble remote controls, with buttons that can be used in mid-air. All these aim to reduce or cut out the need to press down on a control.

If the solution is going to include a keyboard and/or mouse, of whatever form, then other ergonomic aids must be considered – wrist rests come in all shapes and sizes, from a built-in rest in front of the keyboard (or a loose foam or rubber one) to something that looks like a sling on which to rest the lower arm for comfort. Sometimes these are free-standing and sometimes they are on a bracket attached to the desk, so that the user's arm may swing round from mouse to keyboard without undue movement.

The most obvious solution is to remove the need for typing or using a mouse at all, and this is most likely made possible by the use of a voice input package that allows the user to control and input data by voice. The best known of these software packages is Dragon Naturally Speaking, which claims a 99 per cent accuracy level when used with generic office packages. This obviously has the benefit of drastically reducing any typing needed.

In order to adapt a specialist software package such as Rational Rose for use with Dragon Naturally Speaking, around 2 days must be spent creating the 'rules' by which it will work. Once this is done, then the claim is for over 90 per cent accuracy of command and input.

The use of a voice-activated software package will bring its own requirements for hardware – a microphone or headset and microphone are essential equipment. These can be wired or wireless. This may also mean there is a need to soundproof the work area. There is no direct need for sound output in this case; however, the software accepting voice input may be sensitive to background and ambient noise and get confused.

The whole working environment will need to be addressed and there are many choices for furniture, such as adjustable desks and ergonomic chairs and stools to encourage proper sitting position for back, arms and wrists.

A further aspect of the problem is how Susan can continue to takes notes whilst conducting analyses such as observations and interviews. Digital dictation machines now allow the direct transferring of recorded speech onto a computer, and there are digital voice tracers or mobile recorders that can be connected via USB or Bluetooth and can automatically transcribe the voice to file using specialist software.

That last aspect to look at is the requirement to provide an environment that would prevent the RSI from getting any worse. Software, such as Ergonomix or RSI Monitor, exists to remind persistent computer users to follow health and safety guidelines concerning the use of hardware. These software packages are designed to act as a personal ergonomic assistant that monitors keyboard and mouse activity and helps structure computer use in a healthy and constructive manner, thus preventing computer-related injuries from developing, such as back pain, eye strain and RSI. They promote healthy and pain-free computing and also claim to aid the recovery from repetitive strain injuries. Basically, the package counts the number of keystrokes and/or mouse clicks completed, as well as keeping an eye on the time, and reminds the user that it is time to take a break, even going so far as to lock the computer for a set period of time.

The recommendation

Firstly, the working environment must be set up correctly for Susan. Her workstation must conform to all the best practice. A moveable and controllable arm and wrist rest are needed to support her arms and wrists on those occasions when she has to use the keyboard and/or mouse for input.

Voice input software is needed, plus an associated input device – a wireless enabled headset would give some privacy and flexibility, rather than having to speak into a fixed microphone. It is worth taking the time to adapt the voice recognition software for the specialist software that she uses as this will save her many injury-worsening typing hours.

Equipping the analyst with a portable voice tracer or dictaphone to record notes on the move is also recommended. Not only does this provide her with easy note-taking in the field, it also means that the notes can be instantly downloaded, transcribed and used on her return to the office.

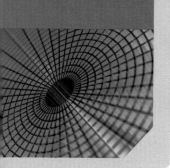

2.5 A visually-impaired student in a college environment

Current situation

Joseph Lewis is starting a 2-year diploma course in IT at his local college in September. He is completely blind in one eye and has limited vision in the other, the result of an illness suffered as a baby. He has no other disabilities. He has attended a specialist school for the blind since the age of 7, where all the facilities are geared towards the special requirements of the students. He can read and write in Braille and his previous interactions with computers have been mainly through a Braille keyboard and Braille printouts, with a support assistant reading out from the screen anything he couldn't see with a magnifier. He gained eight good GCSEs in year 11 and is determined to succeed in the mainstream educational world.

This is the first time that the IT department at the college have had a student with these special needs on a mainstream course and they are anxious to know how they will be able to help Joseph get the most from his course. The lecturers who will be teaching him need to know what extra software or hardware they will need to use and if there is any equipment that the department needs to provide for Joseph.

In summary – the requirements are:

1 a method of providing lectures and notes that will be usable

2 a method for Joseph to independently follow exercises, etc. on the computer

3 a method to safely complete practical exercises with hardware

4 a method for him to get around the college without fuss

5 procedures for ensuring that health and safety criteria are met.

Things to ponder

- Anything that the lecturers produce can normally be printed or projected using larger fonts, but what about text books or source material taken from books and magazines, etc?

- Class timetabling may need rearranging if the college is a split site or classes are held in different buildings – will all theory lessons have to be in one room?

- Should the college designate one PC in each IT classroom used by Joseph for his use, or have a solution that can be used on any PC? Do all PCs have USB connections available?

Possible approaches to implementation

There are sound and vision options available that would allow Joseph to access lecture notes. There are two sound options – the lecturer could pre-record the notes, in the same way as a talking book, that Joseph could take away, or Joseph could take a digital dictaphone or digital voice tracer into the classroom and record what is said for later playback over speakers.

Any physical notes could be printed out in Braille, using special print-to-Braille software and a Braille printer. This is feasible as only a limited number of lecturers would be using the facility. However, these printers, known as embossers, are very expensive compared to any other printing device. Alternatively, using very large fonts might be adequate for some notes and for projected data in the classroom.

There are a number of magnifying devices available, the best of which are able to translate what they see onto a screen local to the user. Some resemble microfiche-style machines, making magnifications by many degrees, and can be linked into any computer by USB. The camera is often on an arm and can capture video as well as still images. They can collect images from up to 40 feet, magnified, so even at the back of a classroom or lecture hall, the user can see what is being displayed on the board.

Software exists to convert what is on the computer screen to sound which is then outputted through the speakers (or headphones) attached to the PC. This means that Joseph could do Internet research, amongst other things, in the same way as his classmates, without help. The software reads web page content aloud, including word-processed and pdf documents and the word it is reading is highlighted. Of course, text can also be magnified on websites as a matter of course.

Voice input software is one way that Joseph could produce his assignment work in the same form as his peers. This would make life easier for his teachers and would give him equality of experience with his peers.

Multi-purpose Braille tools are also available. These encompass a 40-cell Braille display and a Braille keyboard for external devices (PCs, off-the-shelf PDAs or mobile phones with appropriate screen readers), and a basic note taker. This comes in a small, portable device with flat housing. A joystick-like, easy access bar allows navigation around the screen display while Joseph could use his fingers to read where he is, on the easy to read Braille display. Some have Bluetooth connectivity to further ease connections. The note taker facility can be used anywhere and can store the equivalent of 4000 pages of Braille text, enabling reading or writing away from the computer. The software that comes with the device allows translations from Braille to text and vice versa.

Large-buttoned keyboards and mice are also available for use.

One other type of technology to mention is to do with mobile phones. There are software solutions for advanced screen reading for both mobile phones and Pocket PC devices based on the Windows platform. These solutions also offer Braille support.

Other technologies are being developed all the time, to enable vision-impaired and blind computer users access to all aspects of modern technology.

The problem of getting around the college could be solved by a number of means. Sensors and buzzers could be employed, though they would be set off by everyone walking past the sensor, which may become a nuisance. RFID or Bluetooth technology could be employed, so that a message is transmitted to a device that 'tells' him where he is, or gives directions in the manner of a navigation device. These are employed in museums for directing visitors around.

The recommendation

Having lecture notes available in Braille is the first logical recommendation. Then, if Joseph is absent, he can catch up on what he has missed. Choosing to use large fonts for presentations and magnifying anything projected onto the board, again, is a simple, logical step for the lecturers. Joseph must be allowed to have as normal an experience as possible, so assuming that some form of Braille keyboard is available to him within college, or he is encouraged to purchase a portable keyboard for himself, then connecting it to any Bluetooth-enabled PC on the network should be easy.

Another piece of technology that would be helpful would be a digital voice recorder that downloads to text, which can then either be read back, using speakers or headphones, or converted to Braille. I'd suggest using RFID tags and a reader combination as a navigation method for getting around college and classrooms, especially in a practical lab situation. Tags could be put around corridors, corners and doors to guide him from room to room, but could also be attached to the various tools and parts required during practical sessions. In this way, he could have the whole experience.

A three-dimensional mobile recogniser could be used so that any object can be 'read'. An OCR scanner accesses the printed information and can be saved in various formats, including large images and text, and the information outputted as sound to speakers. This could be especially useful in the lab situation, as Joseph could simply place each object under the digital camera.

Realistically, to ensure Health and Safety compliance when in the computer lab, to begin with at least, there would need to be a dedicated observer to ensure that no harm befell Joseph. The college would need to budget for this person.

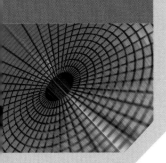

2.6 Creating a newsletter

Current situation

Bowers and Mitchem Estate Agents have ridden the wave of property price rises and made a lot of profit by charging commission on each sale for the past 10 years. The average house was selling within a few days some time ago, but since interest rates started to rise they have felt a slow-down in the market and fewer customers are walking through their doors to buy, sell or let properties. The company has seven employees including the owners Edward Bowers and Ben Mitchem. Two members of staff are employed solely to keep the accounts in order while the other staff deal with valuing properties, sales, and keeping customers informed about what is on offer within their price range. If the current downward trend continues, Bowers and Mitchem will have to cut back their workforce. They are reluctant to do this, having worked together for such a long time; and with a new estate being built nearby, are keen to be involved in any business this may generate.

At a staff meeting, they decided that, rather than waiting for the market to come to them, they should go to the market. They felt that the simplest method for achieving this was by producing a newsletter that will give potential customers the details required to contact the main office and make an appointment for a valuation, or make enquiries regarding properties for sale. They are keen that a sample of what they have for sale is shown in images and that staff details are summarised. The newsletter should be 8 pages long, on A5 pages, and have sufficient impact to encourage people to pick it up off the door mat and read it. It was also felt that testimonials from previous customers could be included along with a link to the company website. Should the newsletter be successful, a regular follow-up may be considered. All members of staff are fairly competent users of software including email, word-processing, basic spreadsheet and publishing programs. They have all been trained to produce information sheets for individual houses by using a company template and have all used a digital camera.

In summary – the requirements are:

1 to produce a newsletter providing contact details and the companies URL

2 to be able to edit and up-date information quickly at regular interviews

3 to include relevant images and detail to promote the companies property range

4 to have good visual impact to attract the potential readers' attention

5 to explain what services the estate agent offers

6 to provide summarised staff details

7 to be 8 A5 pages long

8 to make clear the company's identity

9 to include testimonials from previous customers.

Things to ponder

- What information will go on each page?

- Will it be split into categories, i.e. staff, contact details, for sale, to let, other services? If not, how will it be arranged?

- Should a template for each page be produced?

- How many properties will be included?

- How many images per property will be included, or will this vary by price?

- Will the space occupied in the newsletter by each property be equal, or will it vary by price?

- What specific details about staff will be included?

- Whose working contact details will be included and where?

- Does the company already have software that can be used?

- Are the staff skilled enough to edit and update the final newsletter for future use?

- Which geographical areas will be targeted and how many copies will be required?

- Will the newsletter need to be in colour or black and white?

- What will the quality control process include?

- What specifications will the PC and printer used need to have?

- What digital camera would be most suitable?

- Is there a budget for this initiative?

- Where will master copies be stored, and in what file structure?

- How regularly could the newsletter be issued?

- Which customers can provide a testimonial and how many should be included?

Possible approaches to implementation

To be determined first is a clear and concise logical sequence, displaying the desired information.

If newsletters are to be produced regularly, a file structure needs to be designed to store each version. Also a record of properties used in the letter needs to be maintained. This could be a simple word-processed list with reference details or, alternatively, a database with more detail could be looked into.

The main software to use is likely to be publishing software that includes ready-made templates, including design ideas. However, each company is unique so every effort needs to be made to make the newsletter look like an original design and clearly display the Bowers and Mitchem company identity. The paper size can easily be selected and images, borders and layout options are also appealing for this solution. Microsoft Publisher is commonly found as part of the Office Suite in many organisations, and would be fit for purpose in this case. However products like QuarkXpress, Print Shop or Publishing Express are all viable options. It may be best to use what is already available on the company system as alternatives may require training and may incur some costs.

Alternative software can be used relatively successfully by cleverly altering margins and gutter settings, or individual pages can be created using presentation software, but these options are not as tailored to the task as publishing software.

The recommendation

To produce the newsletter, MS Publisher is a good option and this is commonly used software. However, many publishing packages are intuitive, which means that the final choice will have to be left in the hands of the designer and match what the estate agent already has, if anything.

Publishing software usually includes a range of templates which can be customised to suit the final product. Careful investigation into the layout of the newsletter must take place and rough drafts presented before full-scale implementation is considered. Comments at an early design stage can save time later, when people may change their mind or suggest better alternatives not previously thought about.

The use of images can be dealt with by using the cropping tools in the software, or further enhancement can take place in Adobe Photoshop prior to importing it to the newsletter.

A file structure for archiving and storing work can be simply produced in a range of sensibly named folders and files, which should all be dated.

By agreeing to a standard layout and location for photos and text, the editing process for any following editions should be simple enough after some training or the use of a simple help guide, again produced in a publishing package.

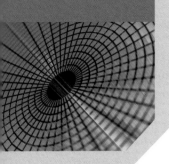

2.7 Birthday thank you cards

Current situation

Stuart and his friends are all in the sixth form at a local school. This year, they will all reach the milestone of their 18th birthday and there are many parties being planned. Being well brought up boys, they know that they will have to write copious notes thanking everybody from their cousin Jimmy to their great aunt Lucy for the presents given to them.

As exams are on the horizon, and the prospect of wasting hours writing the same thing over and over does not appeal much, a quick and easy method of producing personalised thank you notes seems a good idea.

In summary – the requirements are:

1 a card or note for each person

2 words that show whose party/occasion it referred to

3 words that mention the gift given

4 a photograph of the birthday boy, or of the presents.

Things to ponder

- Is it OK to use an old photograph, or is a new one needed?
- Does the photo need manipulation or enhancement?
- What quality of paper is required?
- Should the photo be printed onto the cards before performing any merging?
- Can the card be tied in with the party invites?

Possible approaches to implementation

The photograph could be an old one, used either unembellished or enhanced with photo editing software such as Windows Image Editor, Adobe Photoshop, Fireworks or Picasa. Captions could be added or images merged together to create one picture for printing. The alternative is to take a new photograph, either on or before the night, and use that either as is or enhanced.

Mail merge facilities can be found in both word-processing and database software packages. MS Word and MS Access have powerful facilities (see how to mail merge in MS Word 2007 in Section 1).

The merge data file needs to be set up, with names and details of their gift, plus a personal comment. This data source could be either in a database table or saved on a spreadsheet. The main merge document can then be set up with field tags where the merged data will sit. Other information can also be held, for instance address details, so that envelope labels can be produced as well.

To save hand-signing each merged letter when they are printed, the boys could scan in a copy of their signature and save it for use on the merge document.

The recommendation

Take a new photograph of each birthday boy using a digital camera. Upload the image to the PC. Manipulate, embellish and add a caption if required. Print on one side of the invitation/thank you cards (enough to serve both needs). This way, unique, designer stationery has been created with a theme.

Create a simple spreadsheet in MS Excel containing formal names and addresses, plus names for salutation, gift names and personal messages. Enter all of the details apart from the gift names before the party.

Set up the merge document letter and envelope labels in MS Word. Print the labels and put on the envelopes (keep them in the merged order).

After the party, fill in the gift names and amend any personal message in light of any event that may have occurred. Perform the mail merge, print off the final set of cards and put them in the pre-prepared envelopes. Post.

2.8 Specialist training for four to six students in a small room

Current situation

Professor Hornsby of Burnham University gives training sessions about how to manage challenging teenage behaviour in the classroom. He is a leading specialist in the field of behaviour management and has written many widely acclaimed papers which are distributed amongst schools throughout the country. He has a large bank of resources in the form of diagrams and handwritten notes, which he occasionally refers to when lecturing. His notes are hard to read and, where they have been updated, look messy. Professor Hornsby has just turned 60 and his recent research has highlighted the use of new technology in teaching. He is keen to incorporate more interactivity into his sessions as well as getting his theory across and feels that he can achieve this by using an interactive whiteboard.

His courses are aimed at small groups of teachers who book in advance and attend a session lasting 2 hours. This gives him plenty of time to open up discussions and give the group small quick-fire activities to perform before summarising at the end and passing out key notes. He has a range of worksheets which he often hands out to be done by the group which generate discussion. He likes to keep notes about the discussions and the filled out handouts. However, the teachers also want a copy of the hand out too which means he has to disappear, take photocopies and return. This sometimes takes a long time because the photocopier often breaks down or runs out of paper, occasionally he has had to post the handout at a later date.

In summary – the requirements are:

1 to create a system that displays the key theory and diagrams from Professor Hornsby's old notes

2 to be able to highlight or focus on particular points

3 to make the sessions interactive for the audience

4 to be able to record or log points from the discussion and worksheets

5 to be able to store the completed worksheets and provide a copy for each member of the group and himself

6 to provide hard copy of the most recent version of his key theory to those at the training session

7 to be able to amend and update his notes when new findings in behavioural management are discovered.

 Things to ponder

- What hardware is required to run an interactive whiteboard? How much does it cost? Is any special maintenance or setup required?

- Does any specialist software need to be purchased to work the whiteboard?

- How will teachers interact with the worksheets – wired or wireless?

- Are they required to interact in any other way, i.e. by touching the screen?

- How will notes and diagrams be digitised? What hardware is required for this task? Who will do it?

- What software could be used to display key notes and diagrams?

- How can smooth navigation between software packages be achieved?

- Will the equipment have facilities to highlight key points or can current software already do this?
- How will versions or worksheets be organised?
- How will hard copies be obtained? What type of printer would be most appropriate?
- What level of support will be required to ensure the sessions run effectively with the use of ICT?
- What level of IT competency does the professor have at the moment? Will he require support or training?
- Is the training room big enough to house the equipment?
- How often do training sessions take place?

Possible approaches to implementation

In terms of selecting software, it is clear that some form of word processor is required and the ability to present information is also needed, which could be achieved using presentation software. The ability to store images also suggests that perhaps a suite of software would be most appropriate. It would be wise to establish which suite, operating system and web browser are already used by the University as there may be compatibility issues if alternatives are recommended. Microsoft Office, OpenOffice and AppleWorks all include such tools.

The option to zoom in and out within a word-processing package is possible but may be a little clumsy and less focused. The ability to print is built into most packages and various setups need to be investigated.

The storage of notes and worksheets with sensible file names and a method for saving such documents needs clear consideration.

For interaction with the system, displaying worksheets on an electronic board is the most desired option. Would an on-screen keyboard or wireless keyboard be the best option? Issues with navigating from a word processor to presentation software can also be achieved using hyperlinks set at key points in each document or presentation and activated by touch or a wireless mouse. Both options may be desirable as the keyboard can be passed around or the audience can be up on their feet, interacting.

The images could be redrawn using graphics packages or the originals could be scanned. The clarity of the image has to be the first priority; therefore, the chosen method must display the image as clearly as the professor would want.

The recommendation

The software selected must match that of the University networks and should ideally include the ability to construct a sensible file structure to store the worksheet template and filled out versions in. A main folder called Behavioural Worksheets could be constructed, holding the template, and another folder called Completed Sheets could be placed at the same level. The template would be opened, then immediately saved into the Completed Sheets folder with a sensible name to identify the group and with some reference to the date. If required, these can be sorted later by date so that if somebody requests another copy at a later date, this can easily be found. Perhaps, at the end of each year, a new folder could be created with the year as its name and all files from that year can be cut and pasted into it.

The diagrams can be scanned into the computer then edited, or drawn over neatly and labeled, with a graphics package. Alternatively, drawing tools within most presentation, publishing or word-processing packages may be adequate. Training could be given to aid with this but it will depend on the level of skill the professor has with using drawing tools.

The notes can be word-processed by Professor Hornsby himself and checked by a colleague to ensure they include the intended information. Some training regarding simple word-processing editing may be required. A sensible file name for this document should be established, i.e. MasterV1.

Presentation software can be used to display key ideas in bullet point form and diagrams can be imported where specified. Hyperlinks linking to the worksheet template will speed up the process of locating and opening the document.

A mixture of the on-screen touch keyboard and wireless mouse and keyboard should be encouraged to promote interactivity. Minimal setup would be required and the ability to save, edit and print do not take long to learn and master. The scope to use sound files can be built into presentations, and speakers adequate for a small room would be required.

There are zoom functions that could be used to bring forward the worksheet to draw the audience's attention to certain parts, and some presentation packages allow a highlight option which may also be useful. These can both be used *ad hoc* and are relatively easy to learn.

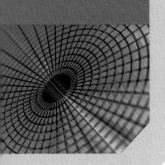

2.9 Large conference speaker

Current situation

Revico offer A-level revision courses in all subjects each Easter time. Large conference halls are booked and up to 200 students at a time attend each course, which last for a day. Traditionally, presenters have produced simple presentations that are projected from a laptop onto a large screen and have had to shout from the front as students work through exercises in paper booklets throughout the day. Feedback in the past has been fair, but numbers are falling as the talk and chalk style methods in use are not deemed to be exciting or inspiring.

Revico need to update their delivery methods to ensure that they offer more modern and engaging revision sessions. They need more interactivity, less reliance on paper-based exercises and a method of assessing the learning of the audience. One criticism has been that people at the back of the auditoria have difficulty hearing the speakers and often fail to become involved with the learning process, and that it is only those near the front who join in discussions and ask and answer questions.

In summary – the requirements are:

1 a method of enabling everyone present to hear and engage with the discussions

2 a method of making the presentations more lively

3 a method of assessing the learning of all.

Things to ponder

- The technical solutions would have to be portable and adaptable for different halls.
- Different sized and shaped halls have different acoustics, affecting what is heard.
- We need to look for bulk solutions.
- Anything for each student must be robust.
- Wi-fi technology might be considered.
- What about interference from other local technologies?

Possible approaches to implementation

Sound amplification solutions are available from different manufacturers that work in a similar way to surround sound systems in a cinema. The lecturer wears a wireless, infrared microphone and their voice is broadcast as infrared light to an infrared microphone receiver/amplifier, which plays through loudspeakers for the entire audience to hear. Some conference halls may already have such a system, but many do not. The voice then overcomes background noise, poor room acoustics and mild hearing loss, making it easier for the students to hear what is being said. The lecturer can talk in their normal voice, thus minimising the risk of voice and throat problems. Different speakers can be placed around the hall, wall-hanging or floor-standing – there are many varieties and sizes, so finding a solution for each room, within budget, should not be a problem.

Mobile wi-fi connections are now commonplace and can be attached via USB port to any PC or laptop. Vodafone mobile connect is one such technology. Having the ability to access the Internet using hyperlinks within the presentation

software could expand the activities available during the day. Access to live case studies, live news or other pertinent sites can spice up revision presentations, especially in fast-changing subject areas such as Media or IT. Inserting video clips, sound bites and moving images using facilities in presentation software, plus the ability to link to other applications from within the software, can be used.

To enable those at the back to have full access to what is displayed on the projection screen, directed magnifiers could be given to anyone who has trouble reading the information. Of course, backup paper copies could be handed out for people to follow the lectures from as well. Electronic copies of all presentations, text and exercises could be given out too, allowing the students to follow on their own laptops or hand-held devices.

Topic roundups or quizzes could be devised with multiple-choice questions. Some of the voting-style devices are now so sophisticated that they allow personalised communication between the lecturer and student. The simplest allow the student to make a choice between, say, four answers, and the results to be displayed from all devices on the board. The lecturer can see if the topic has been understood by the majority, can direct questions at those who may have misunderstood and give the correct answer. The more advanced devices allow the lecturer to pose a question on-screen or verbally, either to the whole body of students or to a single student, encouraging interactivity. Results are stored in a spreadsheet format and so the questions can be adapted *in situ* to correct any misunderstandings and for further clarification. Some of these work on a two-way RFID frequency with a remote range of up to 300 metres, others with HF wireless technology and can be embedded within MS PowerPoint. Qwizdom and QuizzBox are two such systems, but there are many more.

The recommendation

Revico need to invest in some high-tech hardware to improve their market share of the revision class industry.

A portable sound amplification system is the first priority, one with multiple speakers that can be placed in all corners of any awkwardly shaped conference hall.

Investing in a mobile wi-fi device that all lecturers can use with the laptop that the presentation is on, and training all their lecturers on how to make use of multimedia resources and to make use of the Internet is another way to encourage them to update their presentations to make use of the new facilities available.

Investigating the most robust form of hand-held quiz-answering device that can be given to each student is also advised, as this has the potential to make the revision session an exciting and active experience for all attendees.

Like most modern technologies, once learnt and used, the lecturers who work for Revico will gain skills that can be used in other aspects of their day-to-day jobs, and Revico should find their registrations soaring as word gets around about the high-tech methods employed at their revision sessions.

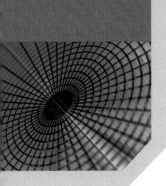

2.10 Electronic portable golf scoring application

Current situation

Brown's Country Course is an 18-hole golf course situated in the Thames Valley region. It has a full complement of members and is run by Deacon Brown who inherited the golf course when he was 45 years old. Deacon is a keen golfer and knows all the members by name. He often lunches with the members who mainly work in the technology industry in a local commercial estate nearby. He has noticed that many of his members use mobile phones, iPods and other such gadgets between holes and wants to investigate the possibility of supplying an electronic score card to be used on a hand-held device instead of the more traditional paper and pencil card that is manually filled in by members during a round.

Sometimes the member only has time to play half a round which means that they would require the option to choose between 9 or 18 holes. A record of each score would need to be compared with the actual score and an accumulated total displayed during the round should be shown. If a golfer scores 1 under or over par, 2 under par or a hole in 1, etc., the system should display the appropriate golfing term, for example eagle, bogie, birdie. Most of the members have a handicap which could also be entered into the system and adjusted at the end of the round when the new round score is calculated. Members would also want a hard copy of the round and hole score printed out. The size of the file used should be small enough to fit on the hand-held device and there

should be a way to transfer it to a main computer at the end of the round so that it can be stored with the details of other rounds shot by the member. Deacon appreciates that this would require two systems and would first like to focus on the electronic score card.

In summary – the requirements are:

1 give the member an option of playing 18 or 9 holes

2 provide a space to enter the golfer's handicap

3 show the par for each hole

4 show the golfer's score per hole and display the appropriate message for the score at each hole

5 show the golfer's total score at the end of the round

6 calculate the handicap at the end of the round based on the score of the current round

7 provide a printout at the end of each round showing the score for each hole and the final round score

8 be simple and intuitive to use

9 be small enough in terms of file size to fit on a hand-held device

10 the device should be small enough so that it does not interfere with the golfer's swing

11 the device should have the facility to transfer the score card to a bigger system on a main computer in the club house

---

 Things to ponder

■ The hand-held device is likely to be a PDA. Which models are likely to be able to run a system which is primarily dealing with numerical data and calculations?

■ Will the customers supply their own PDAs or will the club supply them?

■ Would the use of customers' PDAs give rise to compatibility issues?

■ Is a more universal and consistent system more desirable, especially as it needs to be uploaded to a central record?

■ How will uploading take place – Bluetooth, USB, wi-fi, etc?

■ Will it be possible to transfer the member's round details to them in some type of electronic format?

- The software required needs to be able to deal with numbers and calculations. What are the options and do they complement anything that is currently available?

- What is the par for each hole?

- What expressions are used to describe the performance on each hole?

- Does a record of each performance statement need to be counted up and displayed?

- Where should the running score be located in relation to the score per hole?

- Should the system fit on one screen or should scrolling be introduced?

- Should all 18 holes be on one screen or should it be a hole per screen?

- Is other information about the hole required, i.e. distance and number of bunkers?

- How are handicaps calculated?

- Can a quick printout be obtained? If so would this be direct to a printer or through the main system?

- Where will the central record be kept, and who will maintain it?

Possible approaches to implementation

The options for this could involve using a table from a word-processing package which has some functionality that allows for calculations. However, the setup for this is not ideal and returning messages linked to scores is not a feature word processors are designed to handle with ease.

The use of a spreadsheet appears to be the most logical option as they are specifically designed to handle numbers and perform calculations. The specific package chosen must reflect what is used by the golf club. Investigation into file transfer using Bluetooth is also necessary, although the actual file structure for the master file is not our concern in this section; therefore, knowing that the transfer can be done wirelessly or by Bluetooth is all that is required at this time.

Investigation into direct printing needs to take place as a transfer to the master system could cause delays, which would mean that the printing would also be held up. By installing the correct driver and testing print options, this problem can be overcome.

The PDA used must have and be able to smoothly run the system built within the recommended software. Appropriate memory and Bluetooth capabilities need to be established. The ability of the printer to accept Bluetooth commands is also something to consider.

The system could present the holes one at a time with distance and par information. The score at the hole could be filled in and the next hole loaded. Alternatively, all 9 or 18 holes with par and distance information could be part of one single screen which forms the final printout. Spreadsheets have gridlines and formatting options to allow for a sensible and logical layout.

The recommendation

It is felt that the system should be only one page in length and include all 18 holes, aiming to match the look of a normal score card. The difference in size between a PDA and actual score card is minimal which means that the scale of the solution would be appropriate. The level of detail and number of sheets required to build the 18 page version is extensive and requires a lot of repeating for little final reward. By using just one screen, the golfer can quickly ascertain where he/she has done well and what is to follow without hopping between many pages.

The system is likely to have an opening page asking for round type '9' or '18'. A sheet for 9 holes and a sheet for 18 holes can be built. The Vlookup function allows for the presentation of the score statement for each hole and the calculation features can work out a running total and the handicap calculations. A print area facility can be produced, which will be activated by running a macro attached to a button. All these facilities are available in MS Excel, Lotus 123 or other spreadsheet packages.

A printer with Bluetooth capability and a PDA which can store and run the system can be found by looking at online reviews before making a decision to purchase. The initial system should be produced on a desktop before being transferred by direct or wireless connection to the PDA. Should a member's PDA be compatible with the system and printer, then the option for them to keep the system on their own PDA is viable.

The following link is a good place to review devices that may be appropriate: http://www.microsoft.com/windowsmobile/pocketpc/default.mspx.

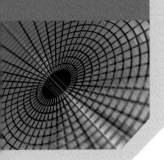

2.11 Purchasing a customised car

Current situation

Pullen Motors in East Sussex sell brand new cars. The customer will select the car they would like and then discuss the specification of the car with the sales staff. The options for adding to the specification include different wheel size, tyres, interiors, lights, steering wheel covers, suspension, engine size and colour. The customer has several options to select from in each category. The problem they are having is that the sales staff struggle to find the price of the added extras or only partially cover the range on offer. They do not use a computer system at all at the moment and record the customer's request on paper and perform the calculations in their head. The only part of the process that is computerised is the final invoice, which is produced from the long-hand calculations performed in a word-processed template. As a result, the final price can be miscalculated which annoys the customer if they are overcharged. Alternatively, the customer is sometimes undercharged which annoys the owner. Also, many products are not offered for sale which means the full potential of the service or products on offer is not achieved.

Michael Pullen, the owner, has asked for a system that will overcome the stated problems. He wants all the options under each category to be shown to every customer on a computer screen. He wants the price of each option to appear when selected and he wants to give the customer the option of looking at different variations in order to suit their budget. Therefore, he will need to be able to input the customer's budget which will be tracked against what is being spent. The final price and items selected should then form an accurate invoice displaying the company's contact details and logo. The system should be able to capture the customer's contact details and it should be easy to print and reset the interface at the end of each order. There are a lot of options to choose from and Michael has asked that the screen be relatively clutter free as this could lead to confusion, although he does want all the categories clearly shown on one screen.

In summary – the requirements are:

1. to display all the categories to enable the build of the desired car specification

2. to display prices when components from each category are selected

3. to be flexible enough to allow different variations to be considered

4. to consider the customer's budget

5. to produce a 100% accurate total cost of the car after specification is complete

6. to collect and save the contact details of each customer

7. to produce an invoice showing the details of the purchase, the total price, and the company and buyer's contact details

8. to have a print facility to issue the invoice displaying the company logo

9. to have a reset facility to start new orders

10. to have a neat and logical structure for the system that fits onto one screen.

Things to ponder

- What would be the most appropriate software for working with numerical values, text and models?
- Does the company have a network or use stand-alone machines, and if so what software do they already have?
- Where can a full list of the different categories be found?
- What is the full list of products available under each category?
- What is the price of each option?
- How big are the screens used in the sales room? Are they adequate for the task?
- Are print facilities available? If so, what are they?
- What price range is the customer's budget likely to fall between?
- What specific contacts need to be collected?
- Where can a copy of the company logo come from?
- Does the system need to be protected?
- Does the company logo need to be included in colour and does the invoice need to be printed in the same style as any other stationary?

Possible approaches to implementation

This system can be implemented using spreadsheet software which is designed to handle text and numbers. By changing variables like the budget or the items that are selected, the system can quickly and accurately update the final total. Some word processors have simple arithmetic functionality, but the prospect of creating a functioning system like this, fitting on one screen, in a word processor is daunting.

The actual production is likely to include repetitive functions, which means that the system will be relatively quick to produce. The main processing deals with addition and some subtraction, and automated clear and print facilities are manageable. The hardware requirements include a basic computer system without the need for anything too advanced, although the option to introduce touch screen for ease of use could be considered. Voice recognition for interacting with the system is likely to be cumbersome and require training for the customer and sales staff. Voice recognition in a noisy environment can also be quite ineffective.

A database could be introduced, but the quality of the actual system produced would depend on the expertise of the person making the system. A database would allow for calculations and would archive invoices. Such a system would take longer to build, but may prove to be a useful source to store evidence of sales. On the negative side, the speed of modeling in a database is reduced as buttons usually need to activate queries prior to an output being given. A spreadsheet will automatically change the final total after an option is selected or changed.

The recommendation

For this particular system, a subsection can be created in a spreadsheet. The actual archiving of invoices requires further investigation and would need to complement the system under review in this section. Products like MS Excel allow the user to incorporate validation lists which, when linked to a source, can reduce the amount of information displayed on the screen. This will help reduce the visual size of the system to one screen. The Vlookup function can be used to return prices based on what has been selected, which can automatically be calculated using a simple addition function. The budget restraints can also be validated between known extremes like the cheapest option and the most expensive sale that can be achieved. 'Print' and 'clear' macros can be developed to obtain hard copies and prepare for the next user. An 'export' macro to send the invoices to a database archive may even be possible, but would require further investigation.

Message boxes can be activated to collect and place data like the customer's budget, name and address details into predefined cells.

The option of a touch-screen to interact with the system is likely to be expensive but could be considered if funding is available. The customers could then happily interact with a stand-alone system while they wait to talk to a salesman. This way, they would have a reasonable idea of what they would like before they sit down.

The installation and file size of such a system will fit on most modern desktop PCs or laptops, therefore the need to update the hardware should not be necessary due to the nature of the system. The system should not be shared across a network in case several salesmen need it at the same time and opening or using becomes problematic. Each salesman should have their own copy stored in their own user area, which could later be linked to a central store.

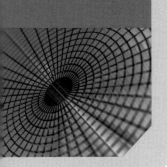

2.12 Magazine competition allowing entries via electronic routes

Current situation

The Didsborough Times is a monthly magazine delivered free to the 4000 households in its local area. Income comes from sales of advertising space and there are articles of local interest. Each month there is a reader competition, which has always been entered by filling in a coupon in the magazine and sending it in. It takes administrative time to open the competition entries, keep them all safe until the competition closing date and to choose the winner. In the past, entries have been lost or mislaid and a postal strike meant that, one month, many entries did not arrive in time.

The new proprietor of the magazine, Jane Andrews, is keen to encourage more entries by allowing them to be made by more modern methods and would like some advice on what these could be.

In summary – the requirements are:

1   one or more electronic methods of entering the magazine competition

2   automatic registration of the entries

3   storage of entrant details

4   the ability to store details that still come in on paper coupons

5   the automatic choosing of the winner(s).

Things to ponder

- Does the magazine have a website?
- What computing facilities does it have already?
- Will it be possible for all electronic methods of entry to be automatically transferred to the results store?

Possible approaches to implementation

A database of entrant details needs to be designed and created. This could be an ongoing store, so that all competition entries over a period of time are collected. Regular entrants could be given a customer reference to save them filling in their address and contact details each time. The details could be used for targeted marketing, or even sold on to other businesses. A database or spreadsheet solution could be used to create this data store.

An existing website could be adapted, or a new site set up to allow online entries via a form on the website. The question, posed with a choice of answers or space to type in a specific answer, could be included, with a 'submit' button to create the entry. These details could be automatically added to the data store. The competition details would have to be changed every month, and the form would only allow entries to be made up to the closing date of the competition. It would cost the player nothing to submit an entry.

An email address could be included in the entry details in the magazine and a player could email their answer in with their contact address and details. This option would be harder to administer: someone would have to monitor the email account and transfer the details manually into the database of entries.

Entries could be made by mobile phone, using the SMS system, to a special number set up by the magazine. SMS to PC software and SMS to file format software could be employed to convert the messages either into email format or to another format such as CSV, which could then be automatically loaded into the data store. For the latter to work, the SMS message would have to be sent in a very particular format by the competition entrant, for instance – <answer>, <name>,<address1>,<postcode>,<telephone>, <email> with the commas in the right places. It may not be possible to enforce this.

An automated phone line with voice recognition is another option. Again, the details could be stored automatically when answering to specific prompts.

The recommendation

A database solution is the best for the storage of the entry details as it has the capacity to relate specific entries with specific competitions, to use a randomising function to select a winner from all entries for a competition, and the ability to quickly produce an input form that would enable manual entry of details that came in from non-automatic methods. Macros can be written to automate transfer of data from other file formats into the database format and the stored details could be used for all sorts of other purposes in the future.

A website should be set up to enable entries via forms in the manner suggested above, as should a competition email address, which should be monitored. Allowing SMS message entries would encourage participation from many who make heavy use of their mobiles, and the SMS to PC software is readily available, with a given 'reply to' number included, and is easy to install. It is easy enough to have a procedure to take the text from an email and from an SMS message and format it into a file format that can easily be loaded into the database.

It is not recommended to go to the expense of a dedicated automated phone line, as the entrant numbers likely to use this method are not great. Coupon and any phone entries will have to be dealt with manually.

2.13 Domestic room design service

Current situation

Bydesign is a kitchen, bedroom and study design company, offering high-quality bespoke solutions for the domestic market. Potential customers phone up to ask for a quote and one of the designers arranges to go to the customer's house, laden down with drawer and unit fronts and work surface samples, to assess their requirements and come up with a design to suit.

To date, these designers have produced hand-drawn sketches, have given a ball-park quote based on the customer choice of units, accessories and finish, and have then taken the drawings back to the office to draw them up more accurately and to give a fixed quote.

Recently, one of the reasons that they have been given for not being chosen to do the work is that the process is too slow and that the customer cannot visualise the finished room from a two-dimensional line drawing. Bydesign need to update their processes to compete with their competitors.

In summary – the requirements are:

1 a visual design tool, for instance, on a laptop, that can show the designed room from all angles

2 a method of transferring all units shown into a price list and a total cost

3 to be able to do this on-site and quickly

4 to be able to print off the design and quote and leave it with the customer

5 for the hardware to be light and portable.

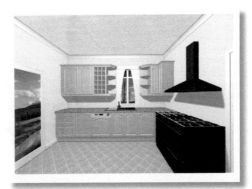

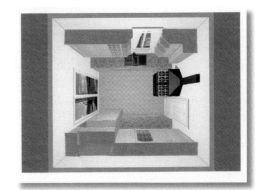

Things to ponder

- Does the laptop need to have a larger than average screen?
- Will it need a powerful graphics card?
- Could the printer be wireless?
- Does the company need the quote to be sent to someone at head office for approval before quoting to the customer?

Possible approaches to implementation

One way to approach this would be for the designer to type dimensions and basic details, including the desired extras and finishes, into a hand-held device and send it back to a central point for a technical designer to produce the 3-D drawings that can then be sent directly to the printer taken on-site. This might be fraught with problems if the central person cannot respond immediately.

The other is to give each designer a laptop loaded with either 2-D or 3-D design software with plenty of predesigned standard sized units and the ability to overlay unit styles and colours onto the design. A printer, wired or not, would also be needed so that, after showing the customer a design, amended with any requests made at the time, a copy of the final design can be printed out and left with the customer.

A price list of all units, with variations for different finishes, plus a list of accessories, such as wardrobe interior fittings, electrical appliances for kitchens and any special labour charges, e.g. removal of old fittings, could be held in either a database or on a spreadsheet. Extras, such as flooring and tiling, can also be held. An ability to create a quotation, using the price list, is required. Much of this can be automated using either package and macros could enable automatic transfer of the quantities of certain items from the design package, so that, for example, when Unit 34 is chosen and placed on the design, it adds '1' to the total number of Unit 34s required on the quotation. Automatic totaling and allowing of extras and discounts can be applied to produce a final figure, together with a checklist of all items that make up the design.

The recommendation

Lightweight laptops with powerful graphics cards are required. 17 inch screens should be sufficient to enable the designer and the customer to see the design clearly. There are many 3-D room design software packages on the market which allow for the functionality described above.

Lightweight, portable colour A4 printers are likewise easily attainable and each designer should be furnished with one of these. Wireless is the best solution to avoid having to connect wires between the laptop and the printer.

The price list could be set up on a spreadsheet application that allows the quotation to be done *in situ*, and the ability to send both design and the quote from the laptop to the head office would be the best idea to speed up the process. Back at head office, this could be turned into a contract automatically and posted out by next day post, rather than wait for the next time the designer is in the office or somebody has time to envelope and post it out.

Training would be needed for all the designers in the efficient use of the new hardware and software. Customers are not impressed by sales people seeming to be incompetent with the tools of their trade.

A further enhancement could be to print out the contract there and then, get the customer to sign it and pay a deposit, and to be able to fax the signed contract back, to get the work under way immediately. This could give Bydesign the competitive edge, reducing the possibility of the customer waiting for other room design companies to come and give them a quote.

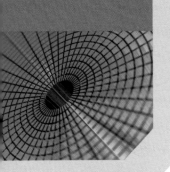

2.14 Newspaper foreign correspondent in a war zone

Current situation

Callum Thomas of Channel 9 News is aiming to run a specialist station that intends to only report from war zones. The trend for one country to attack or bomb another does not appear to be abating and Channel 9 expects to be in the broadcasting business for many years to come. They intend to send reporters to the most dangerous war zones on the planet and broadcast reports, interviews and action as it happens (subject to censorship and what it is decent to show).

Callum wants the reporters to be able to give live footage and commentary as it unfolds. The terrain and landscape which the reporters are expected to work in is often hazardous, usually has no electricity supply because it has been destroyed or removed and is sometimes under a blazing sun. The reporters need to be able to send back images from any location as well as keep themselves and their equipment safe. They are expected to perform one-to-one interviews with serving soldiers in calmer conditions, away from the battle front, and attend press conferences where updates are given. In order to have a competitive edge, Channel 9 needs technology that will give them the opportunity to bring out the news as and when it happens. Often, using an entire TV crew with sound, light and a camera man can draw attention from local militia, who may take the opportunity to kidnap them. Therefore discrete, lightweight

and powerful technology is desirable so as not to draw attention to reporters and their teams. The newsreaders in the UK will rely on reports from the front line and the solution will need to include some way of getting information in article form so that newsreaders can read it out when they are broadcasting.

In summary – the requirements are:

1 the ability to transfer video footage and sound via satellite to the Channel 9 headquarters

2 equipment which is robust enough to be used in a war zone and can be packed away quickly under fire

3 equipment that is light, to aid a quick exit if required

4 that the equipment must be suitable to obtain good footage from news conferences and during calm interviews

5 that the hardware must have a good battery life

6 the ability to take and send still images

7 software to edit any footage which may be too graphic, prior to broadcasting it

8 the ability to transfer articles to the main news studio for the newsreaders to read on air.

Things to ponder

- What type of hardware would be most suitable in the conditions mentioned above? Investigation into digital camera, PDA, laptop, web cameras, sound capture devices and video phones needs to take place.

- What specific features would be required from each of the devices listed above?

- Who might use such equipment already and could they be contacted for advice?

- Is there a budget? If so is it per reporter or per crew?

- How many people make up a crew?

- Who would need what equipment?

- What software would be required to capture and edit video?

- How much memory would be required to store captured footage?

- How quickly would setup and take-down of equipment need to happen?

- What security measures need to take place to safeguard any captured data?

- What software would be required to create and send articles to the newsreaders?

- Will it be possible to use wireless technology to send articles and footage

- Is there sufficient information detailing areas where wireless capabilities are most efficient.

Possible approaches to implementation

A common method for quick-fire broadcasting is the video phone. This device has been utilised by many existing reporters. They are often light and easy to carry around, and simple to use. However, they rely on a satellite link which will be dependent on the signal in the location to be broadcast from. Even in some parts of the UK, signal strength is low. However, reporters are using specialised devices already and it would be wise to find out what they use.

Alternatively, a laptop could be used which has VOIP software installed. The use of this in the field would also be relatively quick to set up, audio can be transmitted via a dedicated handset and images broadcast via a webcam. There are free online options like Skype and Windows Live Messenger which could be used. VOIP services also facilitate the transfer of data files like word-processing and image files which would be a useful way to send information to the newsroom in the UK. The drawback, again, is that if the laptop is not directly linked to the Internet, the crew would be at the mercy of the available wireless signal. The use of a laptop would also give the reporter something to type up articles on prior to transferring them.

A digital camera could also make up the kit required. Some have the capability to film small amounts of footage and can even edit images and footage before transferring it to a computer system.

A reporter can deal with sounds, images and text by using a video phone (also acting as a microphone in some circumstances), laptop, webcam and a powerful battery backup supply for each item of equipment.

The recommendation

It is recommended that a laptop with an application suite with a graphics package be installed, along with a VOIP application. This will allow for free broadcasting from anywhere the crew can plug into an Internet connection. More remote reports, where signal strength may be an issue, would have to be pre-recorded, transferred to the laptop, edited and then sent on.

A video phone with a microphone facility could be used during press conference interviews and a headset could be used when the reporter is talking directly to the studio via the VOIP software. A webcam capable of broadcasting clear images will be needed, which will have implications on the laptop memory size and speed.

All the kit purchased must be quick to fold away, attached to belts or dropped in bags; otherwise it could fall into the wrong hands. Therefore, the laptop will need to have access levels set and all data encrypted. For producing articles for the newsroom, a simple word processor like NotePad or MS Word could be used. The majority of this solution is hardware-based and careful consideration needs to be given to price, durability and compatibility with other equipment used by Channel 9.

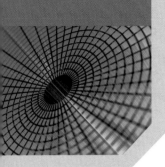

2.15 New-build show home presentation

Current situation

Meerman Homes Ltd is due to start building a new estate in the Midlands region after Christmas. They have four different types of property for sale, which start from two-bedroom flats and go up to five-bedroom luxury homes. The plot is next to other developments and competing construction firms. Promoting on previous projects has always included waiting for potential customers to arrive, providing a swift tour around a show home and answering questions. This is a rather limiting and basic model, which regularly falls down when several clients turn up at the same time. Quite often, there is only one member of staff available to show people around and answer questions while others have to wait, sometimes up to 45 minutes, before they can talk to the sales rep. Meerman Homes Ltd wants to introduce a system which overcomes this problem and stops the clients from leaving empty-handed.

Alex, the owner of the company, is keen to introduce IT to assist with the promotion and information exchange at the show homes. He wants a system which will give potential customers information about the particular house they are keen to view. He thinks that giving the client the means to take information away would also be advantageous as there have been many occasions when the handouts in the sales office for a particular type of show home have run out. Such information should include contact details of sales staff, price, size and plot locations of houses. The available extras that each house could have (kitchen, tiles, bathroom fixtures, etc.) should be included. Most importantly, he would like the system to include images which represent a virtual tour of each style of house. This should allow clients to move between the rooms they select and provide visual detail relating to dimensions and other features like number and location of plug sockets and storage details. The finished system should clearly represent the company image throughout and be accessible to waiting clients to view if the sales staff are busy with other clients.

In summary – the requirements are:

- to include contact details of sales staff
- to visually display the inside and outside of each property
- to include details relating to power sockets, phone lines and storage for each room
- to show customisation options like tiles and kitchen styles available
- to allow customers to choose which room they wish to view
- to allow the customer to receive or take the information away with them in electronic form
- to show the plot where each house will be situated and price and style of the house
- to be on view in the sales office so that waiting customers can see what is available.

 Things to ponder

- What software options are most appropriate?
- What hard- and software does the company already have?
- Will still images or moving images be used to show the houses?
- How will views of different rooms or houses be navigated to?
- Will a front-end menu option be required? How will it look?
- What data capture devices will be required? Is there a cost issue to consider?
- How can customers digitally take information away?
- How will the system be displayed to clients?

- What user interface issues need to be considered?
- How will information about room dimension, power outlets and storage be displayed?

Possible approaches to implementation

This type of problem lends itself to a website solution which can be navigated to from a main homepage, perhaps leading from the company homepage. A list or picture of each house could be shown and used to hyperlink to further information. Rooms could be filmed and played as an embedded movie file when clicked on. This option is possible but would take a lot of maintenance and file downloading of moving images could cause a frustrating delay.

Presentation software could be used to do the same job but with still images, hyperlinks and added narration which is activated when a certain slide is loaded. Alternatively, information could be displayed in a text format.

Both options allow for graphically-produced user interfaces which will make navigation easier. Menus can be added to the side of a presentation or web page.

The ability to transfer the current information can be achieved via a giveaway USB key with the file on. A website could be made available online all the time. The problem that the website could face is that Meerman Homes Ltd may have several building projects taking place in several locations in the country. As a result, the prices for each region will be different. This problem can be overcome, but would require the use of advanced features to ensure that the correct prices are up-to-date and linked to the correct houses.

Initially, a presentation of the known raw facts could be produced i.e. dimension, house size, number and layout of rooms and extra features. The data relating to the particular area of the current build could be added afterwards.

To ensure a consistent corporate image, a master template or frame could be produced for both the website and presentation. A website could be accessed by clients at home whereas the presentation would have to be taken away from the show home or emailed later (provided the sales staff take the potential client's email address). A combination of a website which provides a link to a presentation is also an option.

The recommendation

To produce a system to match the end users' requirements, MS PowerPoint could be used. The presentation could be designed to run as a continuous show or be used in a similar way to a website. Buttons can be made which act as hyperlinks to designated slides. Pictures can be used which fill the whole screen, and typed and audio narration can both be used to convey further details. The file could be loaded onto a USB storage device and given away, although this could get expensive, or emailed to clients who simply leave their email address on paper by the computer which is running the show/system. The options of including a print button would be another opportunity to allow clients to take away further details. A master slide can be made which reflects the company identity and ensures that it will remain consistent throughout the show.

Ideally, more than one computer with the system running would partially compensate for the lack of available sales staff, but this will depend on funds. Laptops may be vulnerable to theft, therefore heavy desktops which are driven by mouse only should be considered. The need to use a keyboard should be extinguished by the use of intuitive on-screen buttons.

Images can be manipulated in Photoshop and audio can be produced in Audacity or MS PowerPoint. The option of using a separate program to make the audio means it will have to be imported, but this may be more suitable for later versions of the presentations, which will need to be edited if details change. However, a single slide can be narrated in PowerPoint right from the start of the project.

A bird's eye view map of the new plot can be used as a starting point. The house in the plot can be clicked on and further details follow. Perhaps a front door with a list of rooms to visit could be presented, which remains on each of the following slides but in a smaller format that does not dominate the screen. Contact details can be placed in the slide footer as well as any other key details on the master slide. Details of extras, in terms of kitchen and bathroom options, etc., can be included where appropriate as a further link from the room where the option is available.

A careful plan needs to be constructed to ensure that the structure of the file is set out logically so that the properties can be easily accessed and extra options appropriate for each house can be explored without cumbersome backtracking or poorly considered navigation.

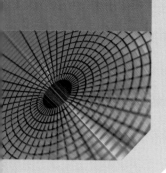

2.16 Allowing for deaf or hearing-impaired students and staff in a school

Current situation

St Angela's is a new primary school being built in a suburb of a large city. At least one of the prospective teachers is deaf and there is a likelihood of some students enrolling who have impaired hearing as there was a bad outbreak of measles in the area a year or two ago, when many local children unfortunately lost some or all of their hearing.

The school want to kit themselves out with the right equipment for both staff and students who may be hearing impaired.

In summary – the requirements are:

1   equipment so that hearing-impaired or deaf staff can successfully teach all pupils

2   equipment that will enable hearing-impaired pupils to understand all teachers

3   any hardware or software that will enhance the learning experience for all pupils, specifically those who have trouble hearing.

Things to ponder

■ What is the minimum equipment that should be in every classroom?

■ Should the specialist equipment stay with the teacher or in the classroom?

■ Will it be needed in every classroom all the time?

■ What are the hardware options that can improve pupil experience?

■ What software will be needed to help with this?

■ Is there anything else the building designers can add?

Possible approaches to implementation

Interactive whiteboards are a must for every classroom to allow as much visual display and interactivity with the pupils as possible. At this age range, there are many learning software options that can be used by all, with colourful icons and simple to use games and learning tools. Anything that is prepared by any teacher can be thus displayed and pointed out to all pupils. Flashing images or words can be used to get the attention of hearing-impaired pupils, rather than sounds. Sounds could be added for extra interest for able-bodied pupils or to

improve the experience for visually-impaired pupils. Combinations of all of these measures can highlight what the teacher is trying to get across.

All teachers need to use good practice in their prepared work – plenty of stimulus material that does not require sound to complete it. Most hearing-impaired pupils will respond to vibrations, so there are ways of using different beats to indicate different activities.

If the school uses a bell or buzzer system to indicate break times or end of day, then visual indicators, such as flashing lights, need to be added so that the hearing-impaired staff and pupils know that a time/activity change is due.

Amplification sound systems could be useful in each classroom to ensure that all pupils can hear the teacher talk. The teacher uses a wireless microphone around their neck and their voice is radioed to speakers around and at the back of the classroom. However, there are more specialised systems for hearing-impaired teachers and pupils to use, with directional microphones and earpiece receivers. One version has the teacher speaking into the microphone and each hearing-impaired pupil having a receiving earpiece. Another has the teacher with the earpiece and holding a directional microphone that can pick up a child's voice from anywhere within the classroom, so that questions can be directed to any pupil.

Soundless communication can also be affected by the use of secure online texting from the teacher's computer to a single, or to multiple, mobile devices. Not all primary age pupils are likely to own a mobile phone, but it is one possibility of communicating with some. There are services set up for this, which the school could subscribe to, even allowing for work to be sent home if the pupil is off sick for any reason.

Use could be made of quiz/voting system hand-held technology. A deaf teacher could make good use of this as it does not depend on hearing the pupil's answer. Likewise, for the hearing-impaired pupil, it means they do not have to listen out for a question and have to offer an answer verbally. The technology is explained more in the visual-impaired scenario earlier on.

The recommendation

Having a sound amplification system and an interactive whiteboard, linked to the school's network, with Internet access, is the minimum recommendation for each classroom.

The school bell system should be installed with a visual alternative to bell or buzzer and a digital, self-correcting clock put in all classrooms.

All teachers should be trained in the use of the high-tech equipment and be given time to prepare learning materials that make use of the facilities available, with usability with hearing-impaired pupils in mind.

Portable sets of specialist microphone/receiver systems should be bought, maybe two initially, to see how much they are needed. One single user set should also be purchased for the known deaf teacher. These can be added to at a later date if necessary.

The quizzing systems are a good idea and are recommended as soon as funds are available. It is unlikely that the SMS messaging system is viable in a primary school.

Section 3

Sample work for INFO1

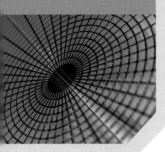

3.1 Introduction

This is a practical unit that is assessed by an examination that will last 1 hour and 30 minutes. A set of sample work must be produced to take into the examination. It is suggested that this work should be about 10–20 pages only. Any more and it will be harder for you to organise your answers in the exam. Any less and there might not be enough for you to use when answering the exam questions.

The required items are:

- a Problem Identification with a list of requirements for that problem, and interpretation of those requirements as Input, Processing and Output
- a test plan and clearly annotated samples of testing evidence that is cross-referenced to the plan.

Where do I start?

Sometimes it is quite hard to identify a problem. This book offers some ideas, but you may wish to come up with something original. For candidates struggling to find a problem to solve, here are some questions that could be asked and some pointers to get started.

- What software have you used in the past?
- What did you do with it? – Make posters to advertise something, make a website to give details about a product, make a short video to give information, produce a sound file to go on a presentation, etc?
- What benefits did the use of software bring over using paper-based or existing methods?

Do I need a real end-user?

It is always better to have a real end-user if at all possible. Only a real end-user can approve the solution – and they can be used extensively in your test planning and test evidence.

Even if people do not use a computer and have an interest that is not computer-based, you will be surprised at how many people could benefit from having information conveyed or processed.

A good place to start is by talking to your friends, teachers or family members. Ask them what interests they have, what teams they play for, what clubs they are in, what courses they are studying or what they do for a living. Ask them what frustrates them about their team, club, course or job.

Make sure you keep a record of what they are saying. Can you think of a way to ease their frustrations or improve their situation by using your IT skills? If so, you have found your end-user and a problem to solve.

What comes into the exam with me?

It is entirely up to the candidate to decide which bits of documentation that they have produced from their practical problem-solving exercises are the best for them to work with during the exam.

The sample work can be from one or two different problems. For instance, the Problem Identification and Inputs, Processes and Outputs part of the sample work could be from a problem that involved setting up a website, or producing a video. For these types of problems, it is sometimes hard to show a lot of objective testing as there may not be any traditional data entry involved in the solution and there is really a need to show planning for all types of data (normal, extreme and erroneous).

The test plan, data and test evidence may come from a problem that required a spreadsheet or database solution, where data is entered into fields, allowing a full range of testing to be planned.

The following four examples are written from the perspective of a student solving problems that could be used for their sample work in the exam.

3.2 Example 1 – Personal trainer website

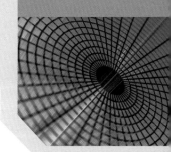

Introduction to the problem

Glenn Jacobs has recently qualified as a personal trainer and also offers sports therapy massage. He is keen to promote his services to the local community and can tailor fitness programmes or routines to suit specific client needs and requests.

Glenn has asked that a website be built which will give him a much needed web presence and provide an initial link between him and potential clients. He is able to offer a whole range of advice, motivation and expertise and is looking to attract clients whom he can visit and work with. His ultimate aim is to have his diary, from Monday to Saturday, full of clients that he will train with and monitor their progress. The professional qualifications taken by Glenn were very expensive and he feels that he has more chance of recouping the investment in his training by advertising himself on the web and attracting customers that way.

He wants the website to show his range of services and have a clear identity which would also be consistent on his business card and headed letter paper. This project will not be producing the business stationery but will incorporate the logo designed by Glenn.

This would be a good project to do because there is a real end-user who genuinely has a need for a website and can provide all the data required and review the website as it is progressing.

How I went about it

Weeks 1 and 2 – Investigation and analysis

I needed to find out what Glenn wanted on his website so I prepared some questions to ask him – a sort of interview – that helped elicit the exact requirements of the website. I also looked at sites used by other personal trainers to get some ideas on look and layout and the kind of features they include. This also helped me consider the questions I would ask, which are:

1 What trading name would you like displayed?
2 How many pages do you think the site will require?
3 Do you have a specific colour scheme you wish to include?
4 What images would you like included? Photos/Logo?
5 If you want to include images do you have any size specification?
6 Do you have in mind a particular screen layout?
7 What other text do you want to include?
8 What email address do you want to be contacted on?
9 What other contact details do you want to include?
10 Do you want to display your qualifications?
11 Do you want to link to other websites? If so which ones?

12 Do you want a hit counter?

13 What would the ideal name of the website be? www._____

14 Would you like to include any animation or special affects? If so can you describe them?

15 Would you like to include any of the following as services you offer? Please tick:

☐ one on one personal training

☐ body composition analysis

☐ weight loss programs and management

☐ flexibility training

☐ strength training

☐ cardiovascular testing

☐ nutritional analysis

☐ post rehab training

☐ in home training pre and post natal training

☐ diabetes prevention

☐ training for clients with obesity

☐ training for clients with hypertension and high cholesterol

☐ sports massage.

16 Are there any other services you offer which are not mentioned above? If so what are they?

Week 3 – Design

Glenn was really helpful, answering all of the questions, and I had loads of information with which to design his website. First, I designed a template to give consistency throughout each page and the website. I started by doing the designs by hand and then transferred them to the computer using PowerPoint because I was just using simple line drawings and the program's tools were all I needed. After Glenn looked at the designs, it was really easy to make alterations until we had something he was happy with. After that we looked into where images and text would go and built that into the design. The position of the logo took a while to decide on as it looked good in several places. The contact details and logo eventually formed part of the template so that if viewers change from one page to the next, they could still quickly see how to get in touch with Glenn.

After producing the designs, I needed to work out how each page would link together, what the buttons would look like and in what order I needed to start building the site. I produced a tree diagram to work out where the links would go and a schedule to work to so that I had a clear idea of what needed to be done and in what order.

Week 4 – Implementation and testing

After Glenn answered all the questions and we agreed on a design, I made the system. The previous sections made this fairly easy, although there were times when what was on the design did not look as good as expected. With Glenn's agreement some variations on the design were made. Fortunately, the site requirements weren't too extensive. For example, he didn't ask for anything too complicated which would have made the final site harder to produce and would have taken a lot longer.

As the website for Glenn did not require any data to be entered by viewers, the option of performing testing to satisfy the course specification was difficult. Fortunately I have a database system I can use instead to show normal, extreme and erroneous data which I will take into the exam.

I felt it was necessary to do some system and navigational checks and to make sure that what I had produced was what Glenn wanted, so I produced a set of criteria which I worked through with Glenn to ensure the site included all of the content he asked for and had the impact he wanted. On a broader scale, testing to see if Glenn was able to fill his diary came several weeks after the system went live.

What is taken into the exam

PROBLEM DEFINITION

Glenn Jacobs has asked for a website to be produced in order to advertise his services within an area of 30 miles of his address. He qualified as a personal fitness trainer 2 months ago and also completed a Sports Therapy Massage course which cost him several thousand pounds. Keen to put his new qualifications to good use, Glenn wants to attract enough clients to fill his diary between Monday to Saturday and feels that a website will reach more people than he could achieve via a leaflet drop.

He offers a range of services which would be difficult to advertise in detail in a leaflet or a newspaper advert and he does not have the time or resources to embark on a telephone campaign. If Glenn fails to attract clients, he will struggle to pay back the loan he took out to finance the courses, and to earn a decent wage which could, in time, allow him to expand into his own fitness centre. Glenn is realistic in that he does not expect a website to bring him fame and fortune but simply sees it as the best way to provide

details to clients who are most likely to want to use his services.

Glenn has spoken to many other personal trainers who have websites and claim that they have found clients who used search engines to locate a trainer near to them.

CLIENT IDENTIFIED

Glenn Jacobs is a 22 year old personal trainer who lives at home with both parents. Glenn has his own computer which he uses for general web surfing and keeping in touch with friends via email and online communities. He has his own email address and a fairly sound appreciation of the potential of the Internet as a forum for introducing new businesses. He understands that many people use search engines and has used sites like Yell.co.uk to find suppliers and businesses himself.

He claims not to be a very competent user of any software other than a word processor but has used some presentation software and stores his own personal digital pictures and music on his own computer system. He has little understanding of how to produce a website or manage a website but is a fast learner and after a certain degree of repetition, is likely to be able to sustain his own site after initial familiarity and some instructions have been produced.

Glenn is the only person who will be maintaining the site, although I will help him if he has problems. However, the audience is potentially limitless and will be people who have access to the Internet and know how to use a search engine to find services in their local area. They are likely to have a certain amount of disposable income which will allow them to finance the use of a personal trainer. They are more likely to be adults involved with sport who are looking to enhance their current performance by using more direct training and focused training methods as well as those who may be trying to improve their overall fitness or lifestyle.

The audience will expect to be able to find contact details like an email address and mobile phone number. They will expect a quick reply and some details relating to prices so that they can make up their minds as to whether to use Glenn or not. They will also want assurances that Glenn knows what he is doing and is suitably qualified. Visitors to the site will want to be able to navigate through the pages with ease, identify details about the services on offer and not have to read through too much text to find the information which may be of interest.

CLIENT REQUIREMENTS

Glenn has requested a website be built. For it to satisfy his needs it must include or do the following:

1 Display the Trading Name – Perfect Fit

2 Be a website with only two pages to display the services on offer

3 The colour scheme should only include white, black and deep red as this matches the kit Glenn wears for training

4 The Perfect Fit logo should be displayed on each page

5 Space for images in the future has been requested

6 The layout of the screen should be simple and uncluttered

7 Text showing the title of each service and prices should be included

8 The email and contact details should be included on every page

9 Details of Glenn's training and qualification should be shown

10 The URL to the site, if available, should be www.perfectfit.co.uk

11 No special effects or animation were requested.

INPUTS

Glenn asked that this logo appear on each page of the site.

The following services need to be listed:

- sports massage
- one on one personal training
- body composition analysis
- weight loss programs and management
- flexibility training
- strength training
- cardiovascular testing
- nutritional analysis
- post rehab training
- in home training pre and post natal training
- diabetes prevention
- training for clients with obesity
- training for clients with hypertension and high cholesterol.

The following contact details need to be present on every page.

Mobile: 07809627311

Email: glennj1973@yahoo.co.uk

He has also asked that prices be shown and some minor details relating to sports therapy massage and personal trainer fees:

Sports Massage Therapy
To repair ligaments or muscle damage
Support recovery after extensive exercise
Aid relaxation after workout routines
1/2 hour £27.00 or 1 hour £39.00

All other services combine under the Personal Trainer Programme and are agreed after consultation. 1 hour £37.00

PROCESSES

Web page 1 construction

- » Add logo at left
- » Add logo at right
- » Add title, location and contact details
- » Add email address and hyperlink to load mail package
- » Add internal link to second page.

Web page 2 construction

- » Add logo at left
- » Add logo at right
- » Add title, location and contact details
- » Add email address and hyperlink to load mail package
- » Add services text.

The services are not to be linked to other pages but Glenn has asked for an arched design from which the services should run on the left hand side of the screen. The right hand side should give price details. All contact details need to be in black and bold, while services are displayed in a deep red (one of Glenn's training colours).

The complete site will have to be broadcast to the Internet using FTP software and include features which will allow search engines to find it. Crawlers used by some search engines do not always find new sites straight away so this may be quite a challenge.

The layout of the site will be fairly simple and borderless tables will be used to arrange the data in various places in the site. The images used can be adjusted while on-screen to ensure that they fit the 15 inch minimum requirement.

OUTPUTS

The system needs to be displayed on a screen which allows the contents of each page to be viewed on a 15 inch monitor without scrolling. The data from the input section must be included and text should not be obscured by images.

The colour scheme to use is largely a white background, black text for the contact details and deep red for the services. The contact details should be shown on each page.

It is likely that there will only be two pages, with space for images to be placed at a later date when clients have been acquired.

There is no need for any audio to be heard or moving images to be displayed.

Details on-screen should be printable by using the browser print selection options, should the viewer wish to obtain a hard copy.

HARDWARE AND SOFTWARE REQUIREMENTS FOR DEVELOPER

The hardware required to produce the system is a computer system, which could be a laptop with a glide pad or a desktop with mouse and keyboard.

The images will be captured using a digital camera which can be downloaded and manipulated into the required size. Glenn has his own camera on his mobile phone but as yet has no clients to picture and only one image of himself.

The system will need to have Internet connectivity for uploading the completed site. The system used in this instance is the Packard Bell iMedia 2410 and 19 inch PB Widescreen TFT Monitor. It is categorised as a home PC and as part of the package a wireless router was also purchased, which means the machine can be connected to the Internet without having to be hard-wired into any one location.

Also required is a 2GB USB storage key which can be used to transfer the site between locations where it can be worked upon.

The software to be used is Microsoft FrontPage. I could have used Adobe Dreamweaver but Frontpage is a better option in this case because the school and home systems involved are still running Office 2003 and therefore the work can be transferred by a USB storage device (2GB) and worked on further at home. FrontPage has table build facility to provide assistance with laying out the page, font formatting tools and an easy to use hyperlink feature.

The system will be secured while online during the FTP process by Norton 360 Virus protection.

Microsoft Publisher will be used to produce the logo and may be used again if further simple graphic work is required. If I had the Creative Suite that includes Dreamweaver, I could also have used Flash for the logo, but it would be too costly to buy simply for one project.

Any pictures of clients from Glenn can be enhanced through Photoshop. Sections can be edited out, the whole image colour and contrast can be changed, as well as blending other colours together to create alternative effects.

HARDWARE AND SOFTWARE REQUIREMENTS FOR USER

To view the system, a modern standard home computer system which has a connection to the Internet should be sufficient.

A mouse, keyboard and screen over 15 inches will help to view and interact with the site in terms of communicating with Glenn.

Should a viewer wish to print any of the content they will need a printer. There is no particular need for it to be colour if the text is required to be read somewhere other than from the computer screen.

The browser the system will be tested on is Internet Explorer Version 7 although alternatives like Firefox, Netscape and Mozilla should also allow viewers to see the page.

EVALUATION CRITERIA

1 Can the site be found quickly on a search engine?

2 Does it fit the screen size specification provided?

3 Can it be easily updated should new qualifications be acquired or contact details change?

The timings and research of the project should also be evaluated. The initial planning stage was crucial in determining what data and formats to use and it will be interesting to note how long the final site will take to build.

The positioning and obviousness of hyperlinks and space available for further images should be looked at, as well as:

1 how well the trading name has been displayed and if the number of pages used is appropriate

2 the colour scheme

3 the impact of the logo and general screen layout

4 the quality of the text data used as well as its screen location

5 the usefulness of the domain name proposed in terms of how easily it can be remembered and how relevant to the business it is.

TESTING PLAN

The viewers to this system are not required to enter any data. They are only supposed to view the contents and hopefully make the decision to contact Glenn using the details provided. The site is likely to represent the foundations for a system which can be added to or adapted as the business grows. During the editing phase, the view of the services and positioning of the text will need to be tested as well as the general use of the available screen size specified. The tests for normal, extreme and erroneous data will be difficult to achieve in this instance and instead a check list has been produced in order to test that the website produced matches the requirements detailed earlier.

Test no.	Test description	Expected outcome
1	Display the Trading Name – Perfect Fit	This should appear on each page and be clearly visible.
2	Be a website with only 2 pages to display the services on offer.	The website should only be 2 pages.
3	The colour scheme should only include white, black and deep red as this matches the kit Glenn wears for training.	No other colours apart from those stated should dominate the screen.
4	The Perfect Fit logo should be displayed on each page.	This should appear on each page and be clearly visible.
5	Space for images in the future has been requested.	There should be space provided which can easily be populated for 3 further images: 2 on the homepage and 1 on the services page.
6	The layout of the screen should be simple and uncluttered.	Services and other data should be easy to locate, and the screen must not have a confusing view.
7	Text showing the title of each service and prices should be included.	Services and prices for each should be on display and easy to view.
8	The ability to email Glenn from the site should be possible.	The email and contact details should be included on every page.
9	Details of Glenn's training and qualifications should be shown.	This should appear on each page and be clearly visible.
10	The URL to the site if available should be www.perfectfit.co.uk.	www.perfectfit.co.uk is purchased.
11	Glenn is satisfied with the site as an introduction to his business.	Glenn is happy and prepared to allow the site to be uploaded.
12	It should be possible to view the site without scrolling on a 15 inch screen.	The site can be viewed on a 15 inch screen.
13	Does the navigation work?	The links from the Index and back work.

Testing

Test no.	Test description	Expected outcome	Actual outcome	Corrective action/ recommendations
1	Display the Trading Name – Perfect Fit.	This should appear on each page and be clearly visible.	Perfect Fit appears on the homepage and the services page in the centre. See screenshots A and B.	None.

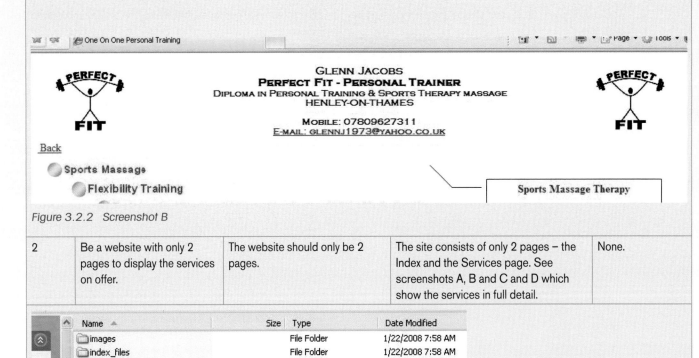

Figure 3.2.1   Screenshot A

Figure 3.2.2   Screenshot B

2	Be a website with only 2 pages to display the services on offer.	The website should only be 2 pages.	The site consists of only 2 pages – the Index and the Services page. See screenshots A, B and C and D which show the services in full detail.	None.

Figure 3.2.3   Screenshot C

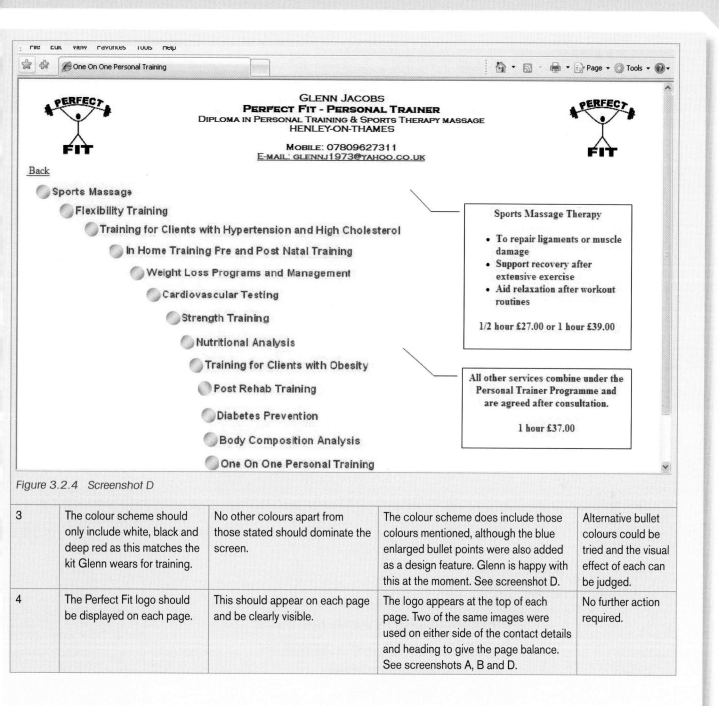

Figure 3.2.4   Screenshot D

3	The colour scheme should only include white, black and deep red as this matches the kit Glenn wears for training.	No other colours apart from those stated should dominate the screen.	The colour scheme does include those colours mentioned, although the blue enlarged bullet points were also added as a design feature. Glenn is happy with this at the moment. See screenshot D.	Alternative bullet colours could be tried and the visual effect of each can be judged.
4	The Perfect Fit logo should be displayed on each page.	This should appear on each page and be clearly visible.	The logo appears at the top of each page. Two of the same images were used on either side of the contact details and heading to give the page balance. See screenshots A, B and D.	No further action required.

| 5 | Space for images in the future has been requested. | There should be space provided which can easily be populated for 3 further images: 2 on the homepage and 1 on the services page. | Space for images has been allowed for. At present, the home page has space under the title and the services page has space to the left of the services. See screenshots E and F. | Images to be collected and inserted after images captured. |

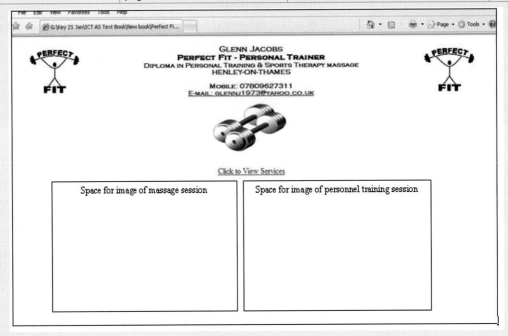

Figure 3.2.5 Screenshot E

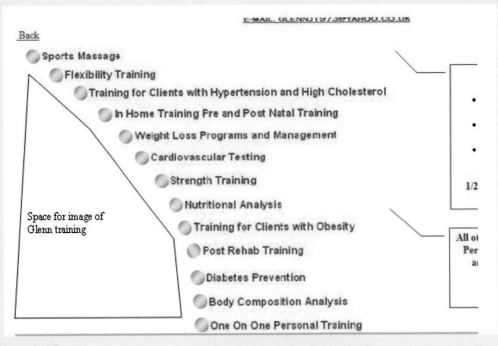

Figure 3.2.6 Screenshot F

| 6 | The layout of the screen should be simple and uncluttered. | Services and other data should be easy to located, and the screen must not have a confusing view. | Glenn is satisfied that the screens are well spaced out but does acknowledge a need to get the images on the homepage as soon as possible. See screenshots D and E | Capture images as soon as possible to fill out space on homepage. |
| 7 | Text showing the title of each service and prices should be included. | Services and prices for each should be on display and easy to view. | This was imported as a graphic and positioned and resized on the page until it fit the 15 inch screen requirement. It was placed in the left hand side of a table so that the text and price information could be shown in the right hand column. See screenshot G. | No further action required. |

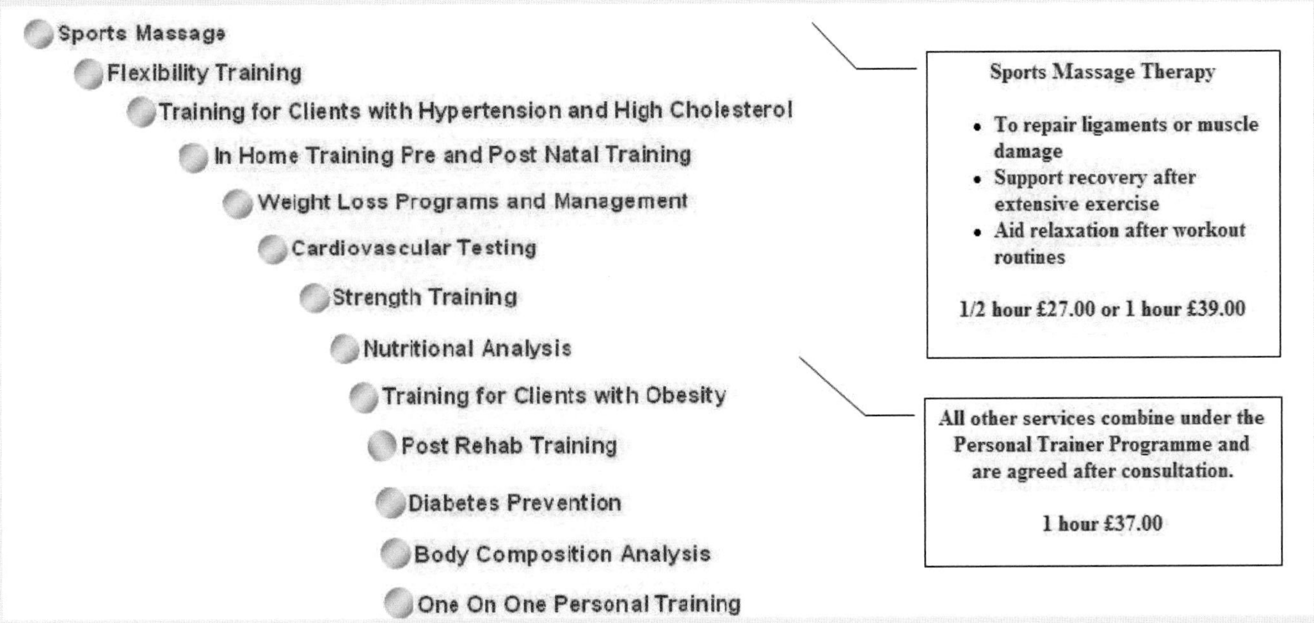

Sports Massage

Flexibility Training

Training for Clients with Hypertension and High Cholesterol

In Home Training Pre and Post Natal Training

Weight Loss Programs and Management

Cardiovascular Testing

Strength Training

Nutritional Analysis

Training for Clients with Obesity

Post Rehab Training

Diabetes Prevention

Body Composition Analysis

One On One Personal Training

Sports Massage Therapy

- **To repair ligaments or muscle damage**
- **Support recovery after extensive exercise**
- **Aid relaxation after workout routines**

1/2 hour £27.00 or 1 hour £39.00

All other services combine under the Personal Trainer Programme and are agreed after consultation.

1 hour £37.00

Figure 3.2.7 Screenshot G

| 8 | The ability to email Glenn from the site should be possible. | The email and contact details should be included on every page. | Glenn's email address can be clicked and the default email package Outlook loads up with his address in the To: section. Alternatively, the email address can be copied and pasted into a web-based email facility. See screenshot H | No further action required. |

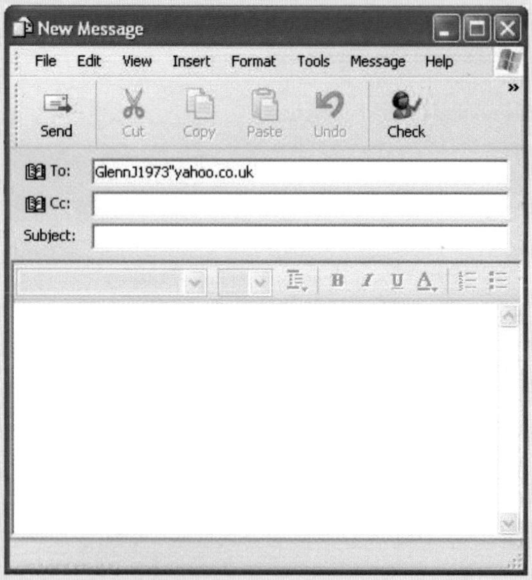

Figure 3.2.8 Screenshot H

| 9 | Details of Glenn's training and qualification should be shown. | This should appear on each page and be clearly visible. | This has been shown on the top of each page. See screenshots A and B. | No further action required. |

| 10 | The URL to the site if available should be www.perfectfit.co.uk. | www.perfectfit.co.uk is purchased. | Regrettably, this option and many of its alternatives were not available. See screenshot I. The following option was found: perfectfitgj.co.uk, which was a close match. See screenshot J. The 'gj' after 'perfectfit' represent Glenn's initials. | Glenn is yet to make a decision on this as it looks untidy. |

Domain search results

Select your preferred domain names and click **add to basket**. To qualify for three months web hosting free, choose Starter Plus or Starter Pro hosting account on the next page.

add to basket ▶

Popular domains

perfectfit.co.uk	taken	☐ Transfer this for FREE
perfectfit.com	taken	☐ Transfer this for £9.99
perfectfit.uk.com	taken	☐ Transfer this for FREE
perfectfit.gb.com	taken	
perfectfit.eu	taken	☐ Transfer this for £9.99
perfectfit.org	taken	☐ Transfer this for £9.99
perfectfit.org.uk	taken	☐ Transfer this for FREE
perfectfit.me.uk	taken	
perfectfit.net	taken	☐ Transfer this for £9.99
perfectfit.biz	taken	☐ Transfer this for £9.99
perfectfit.info	taken	☐ Transfer this for £9.99
perfectfit.mobi	taken	☐ Transfer this for £9.99
perfectfit.tv	taken	
perfectfit.name	invalid	
☐ perfectfit.cc	available	£30.95 a year 2 years

✦ view more suggestions

add to basket ▶

Popular domains

☑ perfect-fitgj.co.uk	available	£2.79 a year	2 years
☑ perfect-fitgj.com	available	£8.99 a year	2 years
☐ perfect-fitgj.uk.com	available	£29.99 a year	2 years
☐ perfect-fitgj.gb.com	available	£29.99 £14.99 a year	2 years
☑ perfect-fitgj.eu	available	£8.49 a year	1 year
☐ perfect-fitgj.org	available	£8.99 a year	2 years
☐ perfect-fitgj.org.uk	available	£2.79 a year	2 years
☐ perfect-fitgj.me.uk	available	£2.79 a year	2 years
☐ perfect-fitgj.net	available	£8.99 a year	2 years
☐ perfect-fitgj.biz	available	£8.99 a year	2 years
☐ perfect-fitgj.info	available	£8.99 a year	2 years
☐ perfect-fitgj.mobi	available	£10.99 a year	2 years
☐ perfect-fitgj.cc	available	£30.95 a year	2 years
☐ perfect-fitgj.tv	available	£30.95 a year	2 years
perfect-fitgj.name	invalid		

✦ view more suggestions

Figure 3.2.9 Screenshot I   *Figure 3.2.10 Screenshot j*

| 11 | Glenn is satisfied with the site as an introduction to his business. | Glenn is happy and prepared to allow the site to be uploaded. | At this stage Glenn is still to decide on a domain name that is available. He is very happy with the look and design of the site and will give the go-ahead to have it hosted within the next few days.

Glenn did comment on the clarity and sharpness of the services list as an image and asked if that could be improved. | Wait for Glenn to decide on domain name, pay for it and have it hosted. If images become available before then, they could be included from the start.

Investigate incorporating services as individual text and bullets rather than as an image to improve clarity of text. |
| 12 | It should be possible to view the site without scrolling on a 15 inch screen. | The site can be viewed on a 15 inch screen. | This was tested on a laptop with a 15 inch screen and fit perfectly after some manipulation of the services image. | No further action required. |

| 13 | Does the navigation work? | The links from the Index and back work. | All the links work from the Index page and back again. See screenshots K and L. | No further action required. |

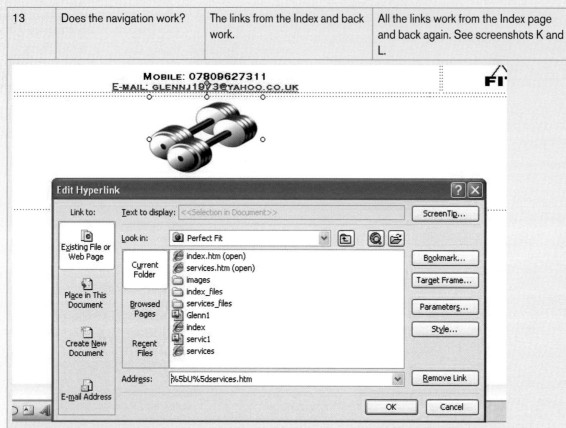

Figure 3.2.11 Screenshot K

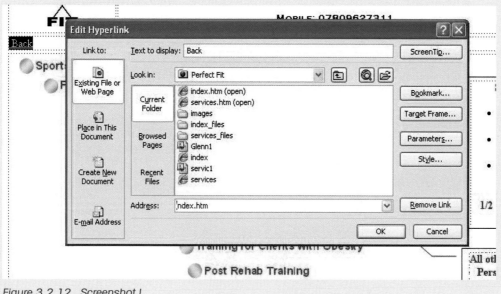

Figure 3.2.12 Screenshot L

3.3 Example 2 – 'How to Scrum' video

Introduction to the problem

Jack Mercer, the Head Coach at Hinckley-on-Thames Rugby Club has asked that a video be produced to assist with the coaching of rugby scrumming. Jack takes special responsibility for the Colts under 18's team and organises training sessions three times a week. He has an hour on Tuesday and Thursday between 6p.m. and 7p.m. and two hours on Friday between 5p.m. and 7p.m. During these sessions the team work on fitness, stamina, endurance and tactics.

The team have played a number of fixtures and are losing key territory because the scrum is badly organised and the players involved are not playing their particular role properly. Better organised teams have realised this and use it to their advantage and easily control the scrum each time one is awarded.

The finished video is to be used in coaching sessions prior to the players taking to the field and practising. There are eight players involved in the scrum and the video is primarily for them, although the rest of the team would find it useful to understand how a good scrum is supposed to operate.

How I went about it

Week 1 – Investigation and analysis

What I will do is put together a list of questions and see if I can find a way of helping his team improve how they scrum using an ICT solution. I am already thinking that perhaps a presentation of some sort might be the way forward.

It was recommended that I talk to the Head Coach, Jack Mercer. Jack has been pulling his hair out trying to teach the team how to scrum properly. At the meeting I arranged with Jack, he suggested that a film on how to scrum properly would be useful because the players could take it away and watch it when they were not training.

I have to produce a list of requirements and clearly explain the problem. I think it would be a good idea to produce a list of questions to take with me when I meet Jack, otherwise I might forget what I need to ask him. I had a quick look at the course specification online (page 10) – the heading I am working on is Analysis. I will use that and what my teacher said to help draft up a list of questions to use when I meet Jack. First, I'll make a firm appointment to meet him.

Question list

1   Forename.
2   Surname.
3   DOB.
4   Position at club.
5   Team involved with.

6 What is the main technical problem encountered with the way the team is scrumming?

7 What long-term issues will arise if they do not improve in this aspect of the game?

8 Who would you like to benefit from the system to be produced?

9 You have already mentioned that some type of film would be useful. Would you prefer this on DVD or VHS?

10 You have suggested that a film to take away would be useful for players to view at home to help them remember what was done at training. Can you explain what must be on it?

11 Who would you like to be shown in the film, i.e. players, coach, fans, etc?

12 A commentary is often helpful in such films; would you like this to be direct to the camera or as a voice-over, or both, where appropriate?

13 If it is direct, who would you like to be filmed talking?

14 If it is a voice-over, who would provide the voice?

15 How many copies will you require?

16 How long do you think the film should be?

17 Films often have soundtracks. Would you like music included?

18 Would you like the film to have a list of credits? If so who should they include?

19 When would be a good time for me to come and start filming?

20 Have you ever used a video camera before?

21 Would you like to be involved in editing the film?

22 Can you tell me about the computer system you have at home and what you use it for?

Week 2 – Design

The results from the interview were really good and I have a clear idea of the type of system Jack wants. He was able to describe the problem for me and will look at the designs to make sure they are what he wants. I am making a film so I had better start by making a timeline and think about the order in which certain things in the film need to appear. The answers he gave helped to identify the data required, which includes credits and soundtrack. The chances are that during filming there will be some footage which will be no good, so I will have to do some editing and learn how to include sounds and add text over images at specified points. The initial phase of transferring the film to computer may be a challenge, and in deciding what software to use I'm split between Windows Movie Maker and Pinnacle Studio 9.

Week 3 – Implementation

Now I need to make the video. I have used some other footage from the family Christmas video to practise and now understand how to get the film onto computer, add credits, crop out sections that are of no use, and add music and transitions. I will need to figure out how to get the finished copy onto DVD but the application has a fairly intuitive feel so I expect to be able to manage that. I am glad that I found time to learn how to use the software because some of it can be very tedious but after a while I got the hang of it.

I shot the video during a practice session and set about editing it. I went for Windows Movie Maker software as we have it on the school network, which means I can work on it at home and school. Pinnacle Studio 9 is good but would have restricted me to working at home which would have caused delays.

Week 4 – Testing

The test plan was quite hard to produce because I needed to use different types of data, including normal, extreme and erroneous. I understand what each type of data is but trying to formulate tests which would give ample opportunity to carry out several simple tests wasn't easy. The best way I found was to go back to the specification and work out a plan from that.

In one of my other projects, I have a much stronger plan and I can use that in the exam, combined with the best parts from other systems. That means I won't miss out on marks for testing with this project and means I could concentrate on the other sections. The testing I did was really only a checklist but I did aim to discover if the film produced was what was wanted, and if it had any effect on how the team performed. The evidence for the qualitative tests was provided by asking Jack for his comments.

What is taken into the exam

PROBLEM DEFINITION

Hinckley-on-Thames Rugby Club play league and cup fixtures. They have several teams at varying age groups from under 11s to the men's full first squad. The Colts team is coached and selected by Jack Mercer who is 28 years old and has been associated with the club since playing as a Colt 10 years ago. Jack's team have recently hit a run of poor form and after being dumped out of the cup competition feel that it is time to address certain areas of the game. In particular Jack feels that the team could be performing better in the scrum. This is an area where games can be won and lost and having a poorly organised scrum has allowed the opposition to run riot over the past few months, causing defeats in matches they would normally expect to win.

Jack is certain that he has the right players and that they are keen enough to contribute towards solving the problem. At the moment, the pack, consisting of eight players, are not functioning as a purposeful unit in their technique and body positioning. They are not pushing as a team and they are not synchronising their movements like a successful pack would in a scrum. As a result they lose ground easily to their opposition and concede points in areas the opposition have found easy to exploit. With an increase in their performance in the scrum, Jack expects fewer points to be conceded and more motivation amongst the rest of the team to match the opposition, because they shouldn't be trailing so often.

CLIENT IDENTIFIED

Jack is the Head coach of the Hinckley-on-Thames Colts Rugby Club and has been in the position for 4 years. He is responsible for selecting and training the players and monitoring progress in the junior teams, where new players are selected when they are good enough or too old to play for other teams. Jack has been involved with playing rugby and holds several coaching awards to prove himself as a credible coach. In his second year in charge his team won the County Cup competition and were promoted from the second division.

Since then, performances have been consistent until about 3 months ago, when the majority of his pack had to leave the Colts because they were too old. Jack inherited younger players from the junior team and has found he has to go back to basics because a lot of his new squad are not very experienced, although they do have potential. It is Jack's responsibility to get the team back to winning ways, otherwise he may find himself being replaced if results do not improve.

USERS IDENTIFIED

The users of the final solution will be Jack and the players responsible for the scrum. Jack is also keen to bring in the rest of the team so that everybody knows what it is that they are trying to achieve and players can concentrate on their own particular area. The scrum consists of eight players known as the front row, props and backs. These are the players who need to improve and will use the proposed solution in order to learn how to scrum better. The solution is to be used as a theory tool which the players are to learn from, and then reinforce what they have learnt by practising it on the training ground.

CLIENT REQUIREMENTS

1   Jack has asked for a film to be produced which includes technical details about how to scrum properly.

2   It needs to have a commentary which provides tips and a breakdown of the scrum process as it happens over the film footage. This is to be provided by the coach as part of the film and as a voice-over, where appropriate, by one of the players being coached

3   The client requires 10 copies of the film produced on DVD format. This is so that there is one for each member of the pack and two for himself. The players will need to take the film home and watch it prior to training sessions.

4   The duration of the film should be no longer than 4 minutes.

5   The opening and closing of the film should have a soundtrack and during the film the client wants to hear the pack working and saying 'squeeze one, two, three'.

6   The players and coach should be included in the credits and the filming can take place at a training session during the mid-season break which is around Christmas time. Jack has used a digital video camera before but is not keen to help with editing, but he will review the film before the 10 copies are produced.

7   Jack would like to witness an obvious improvement in the scrum performance in training and in matches.

INPUTS

To produce the film the data required is mainly moving images. This needs to show the scrum in its formation, indicate which player is in which position, and show how they all link together to make an effective scrum.

The names of those appearing in the credits are shown below, as is the title to be used at the start. This is the main textual data required.

Video Title: Scrum with the Hinckley Rugby Team

Name	Position
Jack Mercer	Head Coach
Gregg Davies	Loose Head
Harry Wilson	Tight Head
Joe Flynn	Hooker
Tom Crisford	Number 8
Nigel Brown	Lock
Isaac Carvalho (twin)	Lock
Paul Carvalho (twin)	Flanker
Ernesto Guevara	Flanker

Jack has not requested any still images, although some of the footage could be frozen during narration if he has more to say before the screen image changes.

Also required are some short sound files (to go over the credits) and the narration, which will be placed over the film when the length of the film has been arranged and the sections to narrate are agreed. Jack and one of the players are required in order to capture the audio.

The sound file to use is Deep Down, which is a copyright-free track, downloaded from www.freeplaymusic.com.

PROCESSES

The captured footage will need to be transferred to the computer system to be used. The film is usually broken into smaller sections which need to be dragged to the timeline and edited. The zoom on the timeline feature is likely to be employed and the use of transitions will be helpful to give the film a smoother look as it moves from one scene to another.

There may also be the need to use other special effects at certain stages of the narration, like slow motion or freeze frame with text overlaid. This will be decided by Jack after the film has been reduced to 4 minutes.

Narration needs to be added after the film is cropped. Titles and credits need to be added at the start and finish of the film.

When Jack is happy with the edited film, it will need to be saved as a movie file and burnt onto 10 DVDs.

OUTPUTS

The final output will be a four minute DVD which can be viewed on any UK DVD player or computer system with DVD drive. It should be in colour and provide sufficient information to enable the players in the team to perform their roles while scrumming better.

The actual viewing size of the film should not deteriorate as the viewing screen gets bigger. The film should have readable credits at the start and end which indicate who appeared in the film and what position they play.

HARDWARE AND SOFTWARE REQUIREMENTS FOR DEVELOPER

To produce the required film, the data capture device required is a video camera to capture the action that takes place in a scrum and to film the footage of the coach giving directions.

Audio can be gathered too, but the sound quality may be limited as it is captured on a personal camcorder. Professional sound recording equipment, which would be necessary in order to gain crystal clear audio, is not available.

As this is a basic production with no budget, the camcorder used will be the one purchased by the family several years ago, which is a Samsung VP D70 and takes mini cassettes. It has playback and record facilities and a flip-out tilt side screen so that the eye view finder does not have to be used for the initial filming. It is simple to use, with zoom control and start, stop and pause control buttons within easy reach of the hand that also holds the camera while filming.

The narration requested can be captured using a headset which has a built-in microphone. This can take place in a quiet room while scenes of the film are run. The headset to be used will be the affordable Advent Noise Cancellation Headset. It has adjustable fitting to maximise comfort and includes a noise cancelling facility, volume control, a 2m cord for easy use and a 3.5mm jack which fits into the laptop.

The system is not going to need a huge amount of memory; therefore the system can be produced on a standard laptop and at a relatively low cost. A movie file lasting around 5 minutes takes up about 18MB of space on the computer hard disk. Prior to converting to a movie file, the gathered footage will probably be twice as long as the finished film and therefore take up double the space. The system will need to have a total of 54MB of free space just to store the film before and after editing.

The laptop to be used is the Medion Centrino 1.73 740 laptop which has an Intel Pentium Centrino Processor 1.73GHz, and the latest Intel Graphics Media Accelerator 900, which provides incredible visual quality, versatile display options, and 3-D performance. It also has an 80GB Hard Disk Drive and DVD Re-writer, 15 inch XGA TFT Screen (1024 x 768 resolution), microphone jack and 6-channel audio out, and 3 hours of battery life which is useful as the laptop has to be taken to the end-user in order to capture the narration.

The laptop has pre-installed software including Microsoft XP Home Edition (Service Pack 2), Microsoft Works Suite 2005 including Word, Photo Standard, DVD PowerProducer 2 Video Editing Suite, Musicmatch Jukebox, and Nero 6 CD/DVD burning.

The software to be used will be Windows Media player or iTunes, depending on where music is stored. This is needed for the start and end credits.

Windows Movie Maker will be used to edit and produce the finished product. This software allows for data capture and includes the features requested by the end-user and comes free with the Windows operating system.

Nero StartSmart will be used to burn the finished film onto DVD.

HARDWARE AND SOFTWARE REQUIREMENTS FOR THE USER

In order to watch the finished film, the end-user will need a computer system with a DVD drive or a DVD player and TV, and, if they want to watch it on a big screen, a projector. In this case the players are to take a copy of the film away and view it individually.

It is expected that the coach will want to play the movie to the scrum pack as a unit; therefore a large screen TV would be useful so that a decent view can be achieved for all players.

Most laptop and desktop systems sold today come with DVD player hardware and viewing software. Windows Media player would be used

to watch the final film although other options like Cyberlink Power DVD could be considered.

EVALUATION CRITERIA

In order to judge the success of the finished system the following must be achieved:

- A film, no longer than 4 minutes, must be produced which provides technical details of how to scrum properly.
- The coach and one other player must be involved in the narration during demonstration of the scrum.
- 10 copies are required to be produced.
- The opening credits and closing scenes require a soundtrack.
- The words 'Squeeze 1,2,3' need to be heard from the pack.
- Credits include players and coach.
- The performance of the scrum by the pack must show obvious signs of improvement over the next few games.
- The DVD must be able to be played on laptops and DVD players.
- At this stage it is important to review how the whole process went and the quality of the finished product. Any problems encountered and difficulties should be documented as well as a summary as to what could be done better if the same task was set again or what could be added to the finished product to enhance it.

TESTING

The table that follows is the test plan which is designed to ensure that what the client asked for has actually been produced. Due to the nature of the system – a film – it is difficult to test the data going into the finished system because it is simply viewed. However, it is important to ensure that the purpose of the system and the content are as requested.

Test no.	Test description	Expected outcome
1	Duration of film is no more than 4 minutes.	Film is no longer than 4 minutes.
2	Technical details of the scrum process are included.	Jack confirms that the detail in the film is sufficient to be able to use it for coaching.
3	Narration is included from the coach.	Coach has helped with technical narration on how to scrum.
4	Narration is included from one other player.	One other player has contributed to the narration.
5	Opening credits include the title of the video which fits and can be viewed on screen at the start of the film.	Scrum with the Hinckley Rugby Team appears on the open title screen.
6	The closing credits include all the players' names, coach name and players' positions at the end.	The following data is shown at the end of the film: Jack Mercer – Head Coach Gregg Davies – Prop Harry Wilson – Prop Joe Flynn – Hooker Tom Crisford – Number 8 Nigel Brown – Lock Isaac Carvalho (twin) – Lock Paul Carvalho (twin) – Flanker Ernesto Guevara – Flanker
7	Soundtrack is played over opening titles.	Music starts at the same time as titles begin and ends before film starts.
8	Soundtrack is played over closing credits.	Music starts as credits start and finishes at the same time as the credits.
9	Audio requested from Jack is heard during scrum.	The words 'Squeeze 1,2,3' are clearly heard on the film.
10	Film plays on DVD player.	Film can be viewed on home DVD player.
11	Film plays on laptop DVD player.	Film can be viewed on laptop.
12	10 copies are produced – one for each player.	After tests 1–11 are complete and alterations made, 10 copies are produced for Jack to distribute.
13	The performance of the scrum improves over the 3 matches following the use of the DVD.	Jack will state how effective the film has been in terms of improving the scrum.

Test no.	Test description	Expected outcome	Actual outcome	Adjustments or corrective action taken
1	Duration of film is no more than 4 minutes.	Film is no longer than 4 minutes.	The film is 4 minutes and 28 seconds long. The actual instructions finished after 4 minutes and 3 seconds. The film overran on the requested time due to the requested credits.	A scrolling effect on the credits could be used to reduce the time, but Jack was happy that the instructions were just slightly over 4 minutes.

Figure 3.3.1 Test screenshot vid1

Test no.	Test description	Expected outcome	Actual outcome	Adjustments or corrective action taken
2	Technical details of the scrum process are included.	Jack confirms that the detail in the film is sufficient to be able to use it for coaching.	After viewing the film Jack was happy that the technical detail required was included. The extra narration gave the required detail as well as comments made during life filming.	None required.

3	Narration is included from the coach.	Coach has helped with technical narration on how to scrum.	The film has narration from the coach (see screenshots below), includes sufficient detail and is clear.	No further action required.

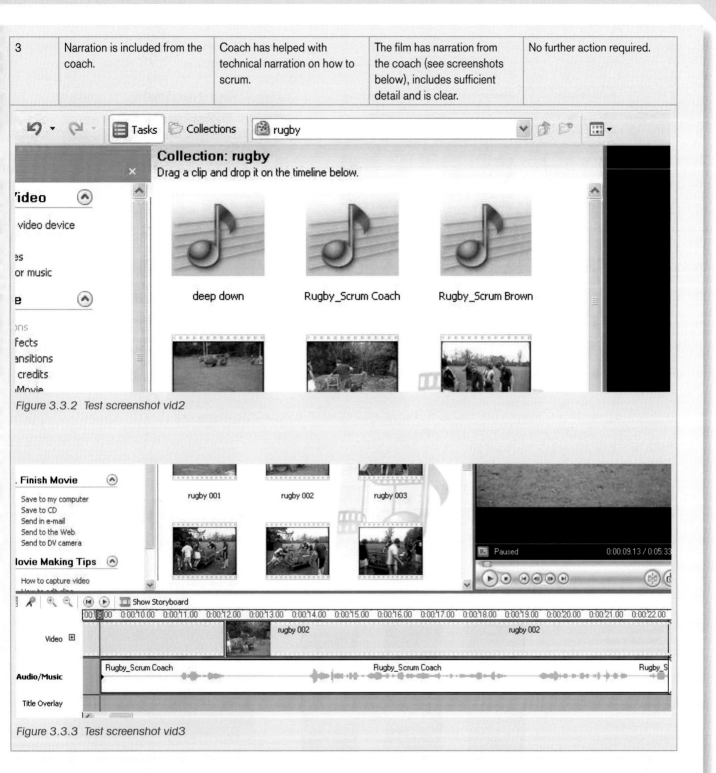

Figure 3.3.2 *Test screenshot vid2*

Figure 3.3.3 *Test screenshot vid3*

| 4 | Narration is included from one other player. | One other player has contributed to the narration. | As above. See screenshots vid2 and vid3 from test 3 and vid4 below. | |

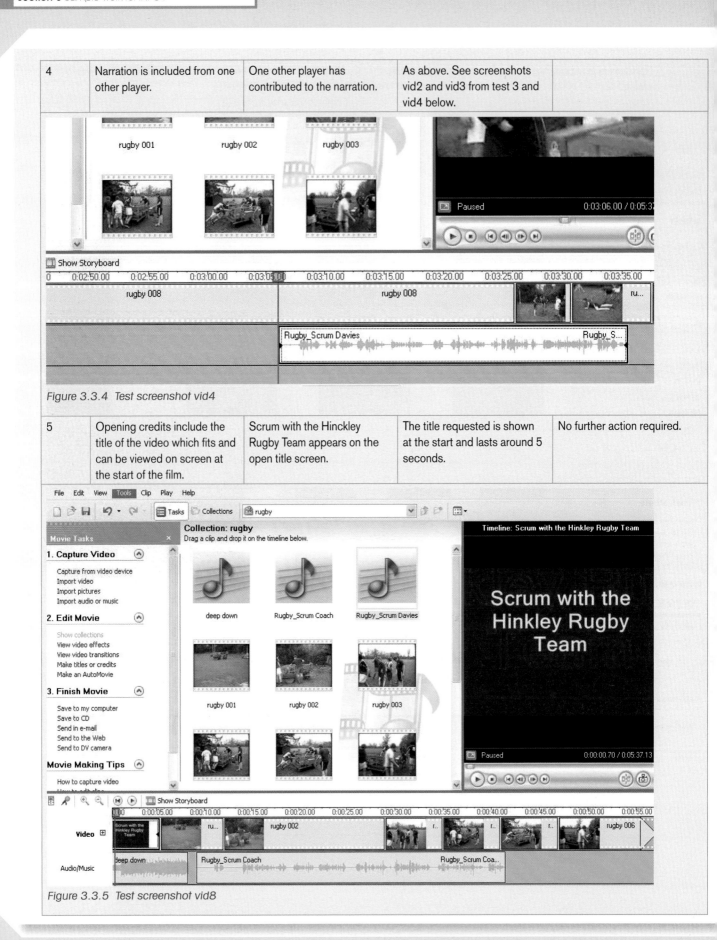

Figure 3.3.4 Test screenshot vid4

| 5 | Opening credits include the title of the video which fits and can be viewed on screen at the start of the film. | Scrum with the Hinckley Rugby Team appears on the open title screen. | The title requested is shown at the start and lasts around 5 seconds. | No further action required. |

Figure 3.3.5 Test screenshot vid8

| 6 | The closing credits include all the players' names, coach name and players' positions at the end. | The following data is shown at the end of the film:

Jack Mercer – Head Coach
Gregg Davies – Prop
Harry Wilson – Prop
Joe Flynn – Hooker
Tom Crisford – Number 8
Nigel Brown – Lock
Isaac Carvalho (twin) – Lock
Paul Carvalho (twin) – Flanker
Ernesto Guevara – Flanker | All the requested names in the closing credits are included with the players' positions. | |

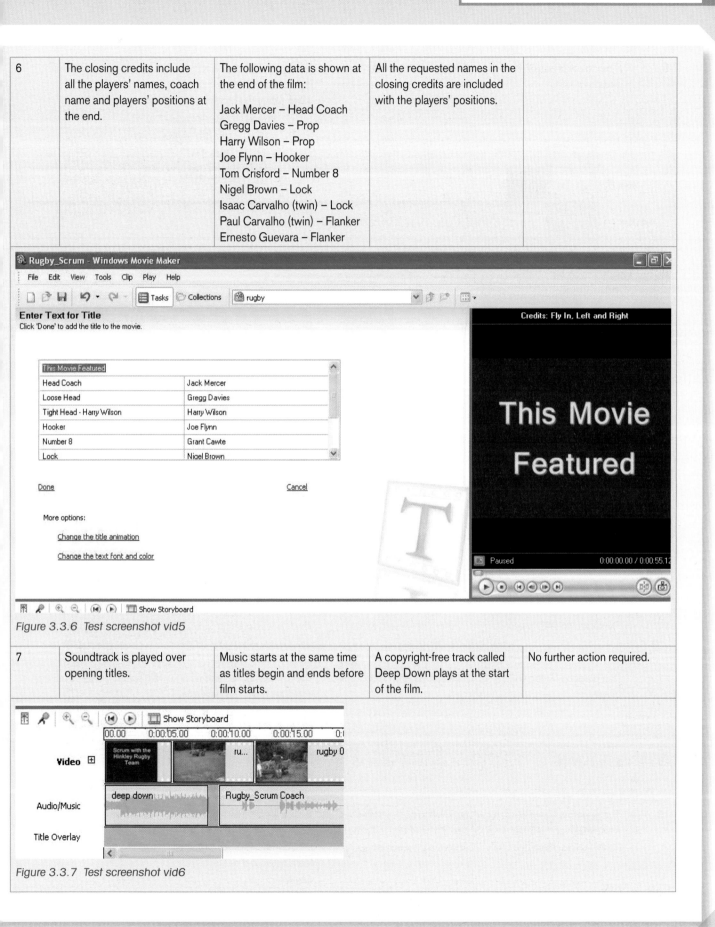

Figure 3.3.6 Test screenshot vid5

| 7 | Soundtrack is played over opening titles. | Music starts at the same time as titles begin and ends before film starts. | A copyright-free track called Deep Down plays at the start of the film. | No further action required. |

Figure 3.3.7 Test screenshot vid6

| 8 | Soundtrack is played over closing credits. | Music starts as credits start and finishes at the same time as the credits. | A copyright-free track called Deep Down plays at the end of the film over the credits. | No further action required. |

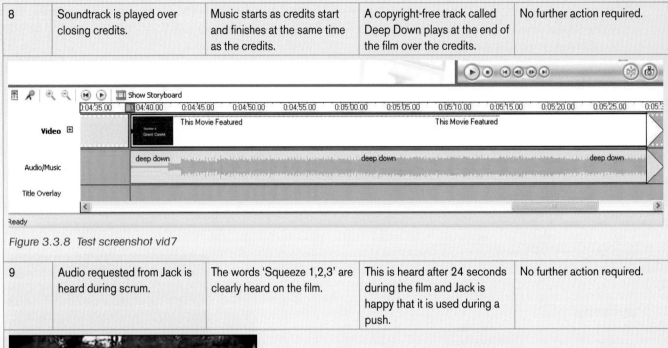

Figure 3.3.8 Test screenshot vid7

| 9 | Audio requested from Jack is heard during scrum. | The words 'Squeeze 1,2,3' are clearly heard on the film. | This is heard after 24 seconds during the film and Jack is happy that it is used during a push. | No further action required. |

Figure 3.3.9 Test screenshot vid9

10	Film plays on DVD player.	Film can be viewed on home DVD player.	The film was burnt onto a DVD and played with no problems on home DVD player.	No further action required.
11	Film plays on laptop DVD player.	Film can be viewed on laptop.	The film was burnt onto a DVD and played with no problems on several players' laptop computers.	No further action required.
12	10 copies are produced – one for each player.	After tests 1–11 are complete and alterations made, 10 copies are produced for Jack to distribute.	The process used to burn the DVD in test 11 was repeated 9 more times. Each player has a DVD of the film.	No further action can be taken.
13	The performance of the scrum improves over the 3 matches following the use of the DVD.	Jack will state how effective the film has been in terms of improving the scrum.	Jack has confirmed that the scrum has improved over the past 3 matches, although the team has lost 2 of the last 3 games.	No further action can be taken.

3.4 Example 3 – School prom

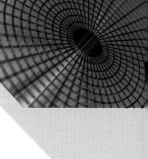

Introduction to the problem

Lizzie attends a local college and each year at her college, a committee is set up to organise the end of year prom. This year, Lizzie and her group of friends have been elected to sit on the committee and they want to make this year's event a spectacular success, having experienced a couple of years where there have been problems, such as too few attendees and a terrible sound system.

The committee have met once to have a free-form discussion about the type of event, possible venue and style, and have had some rudimentary allocation of responsibilities. As the only committee member taking an ICT A level, Lizzie was 'volunteered' to be in charge of keeping records of the budget and all things financial.

Lizzie will effectively be working here as part of a project team and is responsible to the whole committee for producing a solution that could be used by anyone on the committee.

How I went about it

Week 1 – Investigation

After being volunteered to be the financial secretary of the Prom committee, I realised that any solution that I came up with could be used for my AS Sample Work, and so I decided to treat the whole process with some formality. Before the second committee meeting, I did some investigation into what had been used in previous years, and then formulated some questions to ask at the meeting.

The answers I got from this 'round table interview' gave me a list of requirements for my solution. I wrote up the Problem Identification and Requirements, and then I emailed these to everyone on the committee, asking for comments and approval. One or two things were added, but basically they were approved.

Week 2 – Analysis and design

Previous committees had kept some very scarce records, mostly on paper or typed into a spreadsheet with no automation of process. I reviewed the data fields and came up with a list of fields required, along with their sources or how they would be calculated.

From this and the requirements, I produced the Inputs, Processes and Outputs for my Sample Work. I did some sample worksheet designs and took them to our next meeting for approval and suggestions, refining them afterwards in the light of comments made.

One of the requirements was that the interface was simple to use, as Jenny, my best friend and the secretary of the committee, is the most likely person to have to use my solution and she is a true novice when it comes to computers. I need to make it foolproof!

Week 3 – Test design and implementation

I wrote some evaluation criteria from the requirements, then produced a test plan and some test data. It is not a very complex solution in terms of calculations and formulas, so testing is also fairly simple.

I have started building the spreadsheet and have completed the main incomings and outgoings data sheets. I wrote macros so that these could be printed out simply.

Week 4 – Implementation and testing

I completed the spreadsheet and tested it, using all the test data and my plan. I took the finished product to the committee meeting and demonstrated it to them. Everyone was impressed, especially when Jenny had a go and declared it 'awesome' and 'dead easy to use'.

I got the chairperson, Mike, and Jenny to sign a statement to say they had approved it.

I then cleared it down and created a clean version that we can use for real. This is going to be kept on a dedicated USB stick, backed up by me onto my home PC every night and to another USB stick once a week after the committee meeting. Mike will keep the copy USB stick in his possession in case I am off ill. The designed-in change-date function will ensure we know which is the latest version.

Week 5 – Evaluation

I had a tutorial with my ICT teacher where we sat down and he made me go through this whole piece of work, explaining what the problem was, what the requirements were, how I had gone about it and what I thought the result was.

I had to use my test evidence, along with my test plan, to prove that I had checked the solution against all the evaluation criteria and that therefore I had met all the requirements of the client, in my case the Prom committee.

He asked me if I felt that I had produced the best solution for this problem and if, given more time, it could have been improved. I feel that this simple solution is more than adequate for the job it has to do and has taken the skill level of one of the main potential users into account.

What is taken into the exam

PROBLEM DEFINITION

The College Prom committee is organising an event that anyone at the college can attend. They have found a venue and booked a date at the end of the summer tem. The venue will take 500 people and there are 1500 students attending the college, so tickets will be on a first come, first served basis, with no reservation of tickets without payment permitted. It promises to be a spectacular event and they want to ensure it is a success, by keeping control of all the organisational activities.

One way to keep this control is by keeping an eye on the finances. They would like a simple system that will keep track of all expenses or outgoings as well as keeping track of all monies coming in from ticket sales. Thus the Prom committee is the client for this system.

The committee have approached the student union chairman and talked it through with him and he has agreed to give them a loan of £250 to use as a float, on the understanding that they will pay it back when the money comes in. They have

decided to charge £20 a ticket and each student can only buy one or two tickets. They will keep track of who has bought tickets by recording the buyer's name and their tutor's name.

The event has to be self-funding, but they know there will be up-front expenses that must be covered. It is imperative that they at least break even if the members of the organising committee want to keep their heads held high around college next year. There is even a possibility that they may make a profit and have vowed to give any profit to charity.

Three of the committee members are likely to be the heaviest users of the system: Lizzie, finance secretary and ICT student, who will be developing the system and can make any modifications along the way if necessary; Jenny, the secretary, who fears computers and hopes not to have to use it often; and Mike, committee chairman, who is ICT literate and is confident he'll be able to use whatever system is produced. Other members of the committee could, in theory, be expected to use the system, but only in an emergency.

The general feeling is that it should be simple and idiot-proof, but the real problem is making sure that there is control over who is updating it on any one day and that a workable backup system is in place.

The main requirements are:

1   a simple system that will be robust and difficult to accidentally alter

2   the ability to enter monies coming in
- from ticket sales
- from any sponsorship or donations

3   enter outgoings

4   record ticket buyer's details

5   keep track of number of tickets sold

6   display a running total of current balance.

INPUTS

- Ticket sales – number of tickets, student name, tutor's name (from a lookup list).
- Other incomings – donations (amount, name); sponsorship (amount, name of company, contact name, contact details); any other (amount, description).
- Outgoings – category (from lookup list); description and amount; if receipt collected.

PROCESSES

- Calculate balance: total incomings – total outgoings.
- Calculate tickets left: 500 – total tickets sold.
- Operate daily backup process: copy from dedicated USB to Lizzie's PC at home.
- Operate weekly backup process: copy from dedicated USB to backup USB.

OUTPUTS

- Printed snapshot of outgoings to show all items – total and current date.
- Printed snapshot of incomings to show all items – total and current date.
- Ticket balance shown on screen.
- Current money balance shown on screen.

HARDWARE AND SOFTWARE REQUIREMENTS FOR DEVELOPER

- Standard PC with USB 2.0 connection
- USB 2.0 64MB pen drive
- Microsoft Excel 2007 (home and school)
- Hardware and software requirements for user
- Standard PC with USB 2.0 drive
- 2 x USB 4MB pen drive
- Microsoft Excel 2007.

EVALUATION CRITERIA

To ensure ability to:

- enter ticket sales data to incomings
- enter other incoming monies and record details
- calculate total incoming monies
- enter outgoings and record details
- calculate total outgoings
- calculate balance of tickets to sell
- calculate balance of money
- protect data from accidental overwrite/ deletion
- build a simple to use system.

TESTING

Test plan

Test no.	Test description	Expected outcome
1	Ticket sales input and recorded. Use Dataset 1.	Each sale recorded separately, correct cost (£20 or £40) and correct tutor name for initials.
2	Other income input. Dataset 2.	Whatever input is saved.
3	Income monies totalled.	With running totals of number of tickets sold and any other income added in. Should be £450
4	Expenditure input. Dataset 3.	Whatever input is saved.
5	Expenditure totalled and shown on front sheet.	Should be £200.
6	Balance of tickets showing on front sheet.	Should be £490.
7	Balance of money.	Should be £250.
8	Try overwriting protected area.	Error message from system.
9	Test with novice user.	Hopefully she/they find it easy to use.

Dataset 1

Date	No. of tickets	First name	Surname	Tutor initials
15-Mar	2	Liam	Bundy	cd
08-Feb	2	Katy	Rogers	gd
10-Feb	2	Fred	Barnes	gh
12-Feb	1	Joe	Cook	gd
12-Feb	2	Guy	Ritchie	jj
14-Feb	1	Jay	Young	as

Dataset 2

Date = any
Type = Other
Amount = 250
Details = 'Loan from SU. Must be paid back at the earliest opportunity'

Dataset 3

Date = any
Section = Venue
Sub-cat = Deposit
Amount = £100
Detail = 'Balance due 14 days before the event'
Date = any
Section = Caterer
Sub-cat = Deposit
Amount = £100
Detail = 'Balance due 7 days before the event'

Testing

Test no.	Test description	Expected outcome	Actual outcome	Corrections/recommendations
1	Ticket sales input and recorded. Use Dataset 1.	Each sale recorded separately, correct cost (£20 or £40) and correct tutor name for initials.	Macro moves data across from input screen and stores with the rest. All as expected.	None.

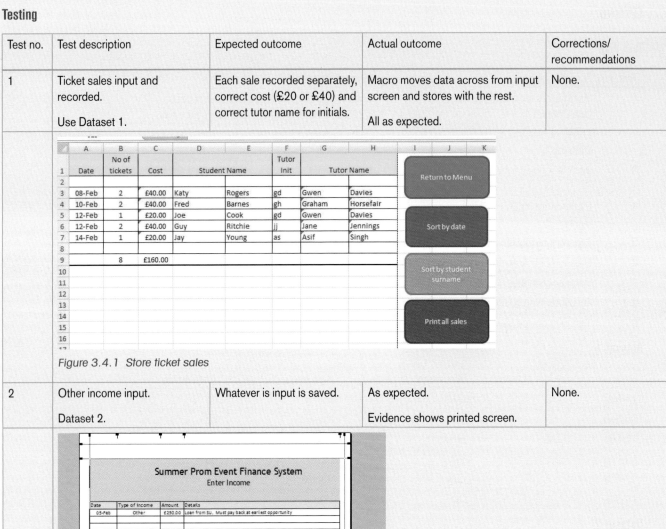

Figure 3.4.1 Store ticket sales

| 2 | Other income input.

Dataset 2. | Whatever is input is saved. | As expected.

Evidence shows printed screen. | None. |

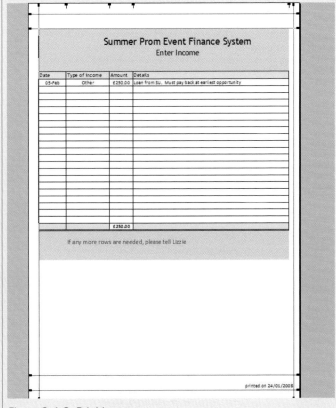

Figure 3.4.2 Print Income

Test no.	Test description	Expected outcome	Actual outcome	Corrections/ recommendations
3	Income monies totalled.	With running totals of number of tickets sold and any other income added in. Should be £450.	Correct – see front menu screenshot below.	None.
4	Expenditure input Dataset 3.	Whatever input is saved.	As expected (no evidence included).	None.
5	Expenditure totalled and shown on front sheet.	Should be £200.	Correct.	None.
6	Balance of tickets showing on front sheet.	Should be 490.	Correct.	None.
7	Balance of money.	Should be £250.	Correct.	Did try before I put the loan in and the negative showed still in black, so had to amend the number formatting style to show red for negatives.

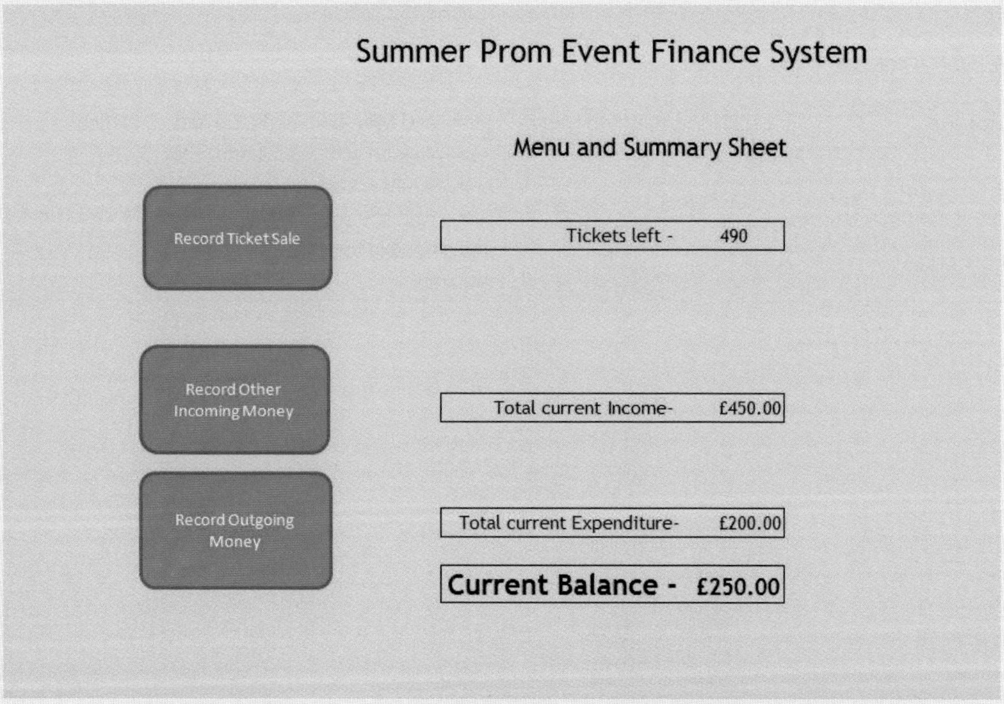

Summer Prom Event Finance System

Menu and Summary Sheet

Record Ticket Sale

Record Other Incoming Money

Record Outgoing Money

Tickets left - 490

Total current Income- £450.00

Total current Expenditure- £200.00

Current Balance - £250.00

Figure 3.4.3 Menu interface

Test no.	Test description	Expected outcome	Actual outcome	Corrections/ recommendations
8	Try overwriting protected area.	Error message from system.	At first it let me both select and overwrite. Realised I had not locked the cells properly, via cell formatting on the protection tab rather than the lock cells directly under the cell format menu – very confusing.	Corrected where to lock cells, then protected the sheet and got the error message – see below.

Test no.	Test description	Expected outcome	Actual outcome	Corrections/ recommendations
	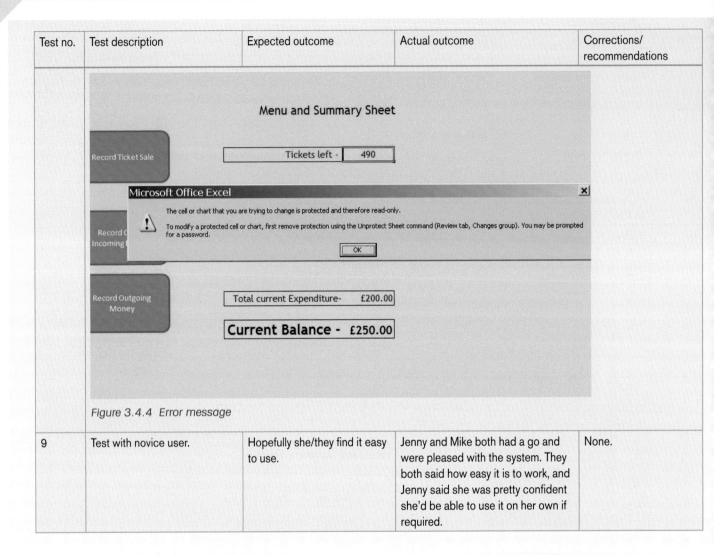 Figure 3.4.4 Error message			
9	Test with novice user.	Hopefully she/they find it easy to use.	Jenny and Mike both had a go and were pleased with the system. They both said how easy it is to work, and Jenny said she was pretty confident she'd be able to use it on her own if required.	None.

3.5 Practice exam questions for exemplar work

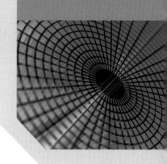

Answer the questions using the Sample Work that you have brought into the examination with you. For these questions you **must** give the page number of where the evidence for your answer may be found in your Sample Work. Also, you **must** write the question number in the margin of this page in your Sample Work.

Problem identification

QUESTION 1

(a) Give the page number where you identify your client in your Sample Work.

(b) Give the page number where you identify your user(s) in your Sample Work.

(c) With reference to your Sample Work, explain the difference between a *client* and a *user*. (2 marks)

(d) Describe what is meant by *an audience for a solution*. (2 marks)

QUESTION 2

(a) Give the page number where you have stated your client's requirements in your Sample Work.

(b) Describe **two** of your client's requirements. (4 marks)

(c) Explain in detail how your ICT solution meets these requirements. (6 marks)

(d) Describe how you would evaluate that the requirements you identified in part (b) have been met. (6 marks)

QUESTION 3

(a) Give the page number of where you have shown the Outputs in your Sample Work.

(b) Describe **one** of the outputs. (2 marks)

(c) Explain how this output will meet a client requirement. (2 marks)

Testing

QUESTION 4

(a) Give the page number where you begin to write your test plan in your Sample Work.

(b) Give the page number where you have started to show the results of your testing in your Sample Work.

(c) Choose one test from your test results for each of the following types of data; explain how the solution has been tested. Give the page number of the evidence.

    ❋   Normal data (3 marks)

    ❋❋   Erroneous data (3 marks)

    ❋❋❋   Extreme data (3 marks)

(d) Explain, using examples from your own testing, how you could use your test results to write an evaluation of your solution. (4 marks)

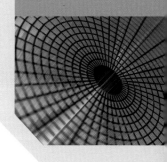

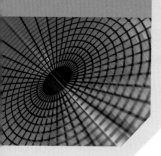

How to access the Heinemann website

Additional web resources

Two further worked examples for Section 3 are available for download from the Heinemann website.

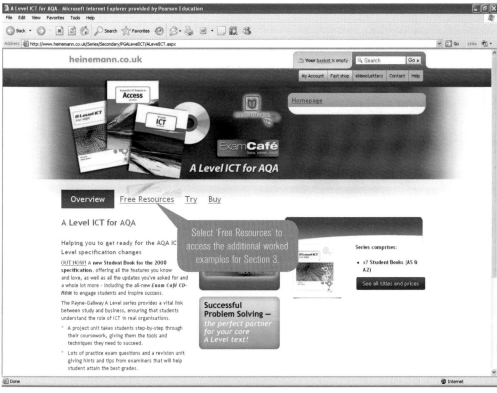